KONSTANTIN STANISLAVSKY

Routledge Performance Practitioners is a series of introductory guides to the key theatre-makers of the last century. Each volume explains the background to and the work of one of the major influences on twentieth- and twenty-first-century performance.

These compact, well-illustrated and clearly written books will unravel the contribution of modern theatre's most charismatic innovators. This is the first book to combine:

* an overview of Stanislavsky's life history
* an assessment of his widely read text, *An Actor Prepares*
* detailed commentary of the key 1898 production of *The Seagull*
* an indispensable set of practical exercises for actors, teachers and directors.

As a first step towards critical understanding, and as an initial exploration before going on to further, primary research, **Routledge Performance Practitioners** are unbeatable value for today's student.

Bella Merlin is an actor and a lecturer in Drama and Theatre Arts at Birmingham University.

ROUTLEDGE PERFORMANCE PRACTITIONERS

Series editor: Franc Chamberlain, University College Northampton

Routledge Performance Practitioners is an innovative series of introductory handbooks on key figures in twentieth-century performance practice. Each volume focuses on a theatre-maker whose practical and theoretical work has in some way transformed the way we understand theatre and performance. The books are carefully structured to enable the reader to gain a good grasp of the fundamental elements underpinning each practitioner's work. They will provide an inspiring springboard for future study, unpacking and explaining what can initially seem daunting.

The main sections of each book will cover:

* personal biography
* explanation of key writings
* description of significant productions
* reproduction of practical exercises.

The first volumes of the series are:

Michael Chekhov by Franc Chamberlain
Jacques Lecoq by Simon Murray
Vsevolod Meyerhold by Jonathan Pitches
Konstantin Stanislavsky by Bella Merlin

Future volumes will include:

Eugenio Barba
Pina Bausch
Augusto Boal
Bertolt Brecht
Peter Brook
Jerzy Grotowski
Anna Halprin
Joan Littlewood
Ariane Mnouchkine

KONSTANTIN STANISLAVSKY

Bella Merlin

Routledge
Taylor & Francis Group

LONDON AND NEW YORK

First published 2003
by Routledge
11 New Fetter Lane, London EC4P 4EE

Simultaneously published in the USA and Canada
by Routledge
29 West 35th Street, New York, NY 10001

Routledge is an imprint of the Taylor & Francis Group

Typeset in Perpetua by
Florence Production Ltd, Stoodleigh, Devon
Printed and bound in Great Britain by
TJ International Ltd, Padstow, Cornwall

British Library Cataloguing in Publication Data
A catalogue record for this book is available from
the British Library

Library of Congress Cataloging in Publication Data
Merlin, Bella.
  Konstantin Stanislavsky/Bella Merlin.
    p. cm.
  Includes bibliographical references and index.
  1. Stanislavsky, Konstantin, 1863–1938 – Criticism and
  interpretation.   2. Method (Acting)   I. Title.
  PN2062.M47 2003
  792′.0233′092–dc21   2003003644

ISBN 0–415–25885–5 (hbk)
ISBN 0–415–25886–3 (pbk)

FOR
THE MAN,
THE MENTOR
AND
S. B. ISUMEL

CONTENTS

FIGURES

ACKNOWLEDGEMENTS

Much of the information in the first chapter of this book has been drawn from excellent books by Jean Norman Benedetti, Sharon M. Carnicke, Nick Worrall and David Allen, as well, of course, as Stanislavsky's own *My Life in Art*. Stanislavsky's *An Actor's Handbook* (London: Methuen, 1990) provides a thorough 'dictionary of terms'; however, a brief glossary is included at the end of this volume (entries appearing in bold in the main body of the text at first mention). Photographs for the Inner Motive Forces and the Adult, Parent and Child illustrations are produced with permission from Vladimir Ananyev and Alexander Delamere, who also provides permission for use of an extract from his play, *Don Juan in Love*. The formulation of Stanislavsky's 'system' is adapted from the table in Jean Benedetti's *Stanislavski: An Introduction* (London: Methuen, 1994: 61) and the chart in Robert Lewis's *Method – or Madness?* (New York: Samuel French, 1986), both of which are based on Stanislavsky's own notes. Line drawings of the production plan for *The Seagull* are adapted by the author from Stanislavsky's own sketches (*Chayka: V Postanovke, Regisserskaya Partitura Stanislavskovo*, Leningrad: Isskustvo, 1938: 118, 135–7, 189, 193, 195, 205 and 295; see selected bibliography under Balukhaty 1952). Illustrations of Stanislavsky are from the author's private collection. Thereon in, thanks are owed to Franc Chamberlain, Talia Rodgers and Rosie Waters for editorial advice, and Dr Maggie B. Gale of Birmingham University's

Department of Drama and Theatre Arts. Finally, sincerest thanks go to three extraordinary theatre practitioners. The first is Max Stafford-Clark, with whom I was working during the final stages of writing this book — he provides rock-solid proof that the 'Business' and the 'Academy' can be excellent bedfellows. The second is Katya Kamotskaya of the Royal Scottish Academy of Music and Drama — her understanding of 'communion' is consummate. The third is Vladimir Ananyev of Moscow's Theatre of Clowns — an inspiring mentor and eternal friend, with whom many of the following ideas and exercises have been discussed and explored.

BIOGRAPHY IN SOCIAL AND ARTISTIC CONTEXT

INTRODUCTION

→Actor↗Director→Husband←Director↖Father→Actor↙
Director↗Teacher↑

The challenge for anyone tracing Stanislavsky's biography is that the path isn't linear. Sometimes he ditched an idea only to pick it up again years later; at other times, the preoccupations of his mature life can be traced right back to his childhood. He was full of contradictions and often an artistic maverick. Nevertheless, this is a man who was passionate about theatrical 'truth'. His evolution as a theatre practitioner can be divided into four broad sections: the amateur years, the director dictator, round-the-table analysis and the final legacies. There are times when the work of the *director* dominated, then for a while the *writer* became central, and at other times *actor-training* was foregrounded. Added to all this, there were political events in Russia which influenced his choice of vocabulary, and various artistic 'isms' (including Naturalism and Symbolism) also played their part in defining Stanislavsky's 'system'.

THE AMATEUR YEARS: 1863–98

KOSTYA ALEKSEYEV

Born in 1863 into one of Russia's wealthiest families, Konstantin Sergeyevich Alekseyev was the second of nine siblings. Along with four brothers and four sisters, his childhood was spent at the theatre, opera, circus and ballet: arts and entertainment formed the family's staple diet. It was no surprise when, in 1877, his father converted a room at their country house into a theatre, where the children produced plays for the guests' entertainment. Here, at the age of fourteen, Kostya began writing up these forays into drama; his youthful eagerness to analyse his own work would, later in his adulthood, inform his acting 'system'. By 1885 – aged twenty-two – his Notebooks were filled with increasingly sophisticated questions: 'What is the physiological aspect of the role? The psychic aspect of the role?' (Stanislavsky cited in Benedetti 1999: 23). Already he had made the vital connection between body and mind (see Figure 1.1).

Kostya's young professional life was spent in the family textile business, although his passion for theatre soon hurled him into a series of ventures, not the least of which was the Alekseyev Circle, his family's highly acclaimed acting troupe. When the Circle folded in 1888, Kostya fuelled his love of performing by secretly appearing in a host of risqué amateur theatricals. To protect the family's reputation, he adopted the stage name, 'Stanislavsky', after a ballerina whom, as a young boy, he had lovingly adored from afar. Before long, the 'Stanislavsky' cover was blown, when his father discovered him cavorting in a lewd French farce and immediately prompted him to legitimise his acting. Thereupon, Stanislavsky undertook his next entrepreneurial project, the formation of the Moscow Amateur Music-Dramatic Circle. Within months, this had given way to the far more ambitious Society of Art and Literature, involving fellow collaborators, Fyodor Komissarzhevsky (an opera singer) and Aleksandr Fedotov (a director). Working with theatre professionals provoked in Stanislavsky a serious need to question his own acting.

AN EARLY GLIMPSE OF A 'SYSTEM'

His first major engagement with the Society was in 1888 with the lead role in Pushkin's *The Miserly Knight*. The experience threw up three

Figure 1.1 Konstantin Stanislavsky, aged twenty-one (1884)

concerns: What were the differences between 'character' acting and 'personality' acting? How could actors stimulate their imaginations and therefore their 'creative will'? And how did actors 'get inside' the director's ideas?

The first concern arose because Stanislavsky envisaged himself as a dashing 'personality' actor, and the Miserly Knight as a romantic lead; Fedotov, however, saw the role as a decrepit old man (see Figure 1.2). Given that Stanislavsky was only twenty-five, this was clearly a case of casting against 'type'. Not quite knowing what to do with the part, he adopted an externalised style of 'character' acting that he knew was really lacking 'something'. This gave rise to his second concern: how to stimulate the imagination? In an attempt to find the 'something' lacking, he spent a night locked in the cellar of a castle. This experiment was his first intuitive understanding of what he was later to call **affective memory**, whereby actors find an analogous situation from their own experience that mirrors the character's fictional life. In typical fervour, Stanislavsky went to an extreme. By setting up a real situation, he hoped that, once he returned to the rehearsal room, his memory of the gloomy experience would provide the elusive component that was currently missing in his 'Knight'. He was wrong: all he got was a cold (and his imagination was none the sharper). The third difficulty in his rehearsal of *The Miserly Knight* was that Fedotov had very specific results that he wanted him to achieve. Yet Stanislavsky had no method for personalising those results, and all he could do was mimic them. Although it was frustrating, the seeds of his 'system' had been planted: how was he to move from external result to internal process?

A production of Krilov's *The Spoiled Darling* distracted him for a while that year. His leading lady was a charming actress, Maria Perevoshchikova (1866–1943), who also hid behind a stage name, that of 'Lilina'. They fell in love, were married in 1889, and spent the rest of their lives as partners and workmates.

The distraction of love didn't last forever. The internal/external acting dilemma arose again in 1896 when Stanislavsky played Othello. One of the biggest influences on his performance style was the great nineteenth-century actor, Mikhail Shchepkin (1788–1863). Shchepkin believed that the key to 'truthful' acting was to 'take your examples from real life'. Following Shchepkin's advice, Stanislavsky found a real-life 'image' upon which to base his interpretation of Othello – it was an Arab whom he met and befriended in Paris. He then set about

Figure 1.2 Stanislavsky, aged twenty-five, in Pushkin's *The Miserly Knight* (1888)

crafting a 'mask' for himself based on the flesh-and-blood Arab acquaintance. The 'mask' was precise in its external detail, but inside there was nothing living, it was just an imitation. *Othello* threw up more concerns for the ever-questioning Stanislavsky: When does an actor 'become' the character? And how does the actor observe life and then turn those observations into 'creative will', or 'inspiration'? Stanislavsky had tried to incarnate a 'truthful', psychological portrait, and yet nothing emerged but a skilful sculpture.

But why was Stanislavsky so preoccupied with the psychology of acting? Turning to the state of Russian theatre at the time soon explains his heartfelt frustration. . . .

THE STATE OF THE ARTS

Theatrical repertoire in Russia towards the end of the nineteenth century was in a quagmire of stagnation. The Imperial theatres (those subsidised by the State) dominated Moscow and St Petersburg and, along with a smattering of privately owned venues, they operated under the beady eyes of Tsar Nicholas II's censors. Their hawkish gaze kept a tight rein on any play whose subject matter might be deemed politically or personally subversive. 'Safe' theatrical fare consisted of melodramas and vaudevilles, hastily translated from the French and German originals, though occasionally an innovative piece of new writing surfaced. Describing his play, *The Last Will*, Vladimir Nemirovich-Danchenko (1858–1943) wrote that:

> This play greatly pleased the actors. It was written as was said in those days, in soft tones; it did not offend anyone and revolutionised nothing; the chief thing about it was its excellent roles: big scenes with temperament and effective exits.
>
> (1937: 12)

Not only does Nemirovich admit here that the more timid the play, the more likely its success, but also he reveals the importance of the actors.

Russian theatre of the nineteenth century was actor-driven: the idea of a director shaping a production was unheard of. In fact, 'The role of stage director was a very modest one; it had neither a creative nor a pedagogic content. Actors listened to him merely out of politeness' (ibid.: 29). But there's no need for a director when you already know what's required of your acting. In a repertoire where melodrama predominated, actors were cast to a formulaic type known as an *emploi*. This meant that each performer specialised in a particular role, such as the romantic lover, the comic flunkey or the bumbling father, according to his or her personality and stature. This *emploi* then became the blueprint for any role that the actor played. The audience grew familiar with both the actor and the *emploi*, and began to expect it at every performance, regardless of the play. The result of the audience's expectation was the development of a 'star system', as 'actors lost their independence and went into the service of the crowd' (Stanislavsky 1984: 105). The 'big scenes with temperament and effective exits' referred to by Nemirovich involved the star actors being 'called out' by the audience in the middle of a scene to come centre stage and receive wild applause. The remaining on-stage cast froze, doll-like, until the adored actor had finished bowing, at which point the **action** of the play could resume. It was the playwright's job to incorporate these moments into a script, and the more famous the actor the more effective exits would be required. Here, then, was no ensemble acting: here was a theatre dominated by a 'star system'.

The situation was exacerbated by the frighteningly short rehearsal periods, which often resulted in actors simply not knowing their lines. And yet it was hardly their fault. At a time when leisure pursuits were limited, a rapid turnover of repertoire was a prerequisite of any business-minded theatre. Consequently, rehearsal time for a new production was a rarity, not a necessity. Quantity ruled over quality, leading to a situation where most performers had greater need of a prompter than a director. To save them from embarrassment, the prompt box was situated Down-Stage-Centre and sunk into the floor. It was not uncommon for much of a play's action to be performed 'DSC', so that the actors could be prompted through their entire performance.

The 'star system' also impacted on the design of a show. Designers were still unusual in most theatres, and the rapidity of the repertoire's turnaround prohibited anything more ambitious than the recycling of old productions. Sets were dragged from the store, with stock canvas backdrops depicting dining rooms, gardens, or parlours, reappearing regardless of the genre or form of the play in question. As for costume design, this was determined by the leading actresses, each of whom was expected to supply her own wardrobe. Should the leading lady choose to wear crimson in the third act, then woe betide the female juvenile if she decided to wear red! An actress's acclaim lay in direct proportion to the voluptuousness of her wardrobe; therefore, money was vital and that often meant relying on a wealthy patron. As one actress of the time declared: 'How could you have a career without a wardrobe. What is an actress without costumes? She is a beggar; her route to the stage is cut off' (Velizarii cited in Schuler 1996: 31). Wealth and wardrobe swung an actress's fate: acting processes were the last consideration.

For all their influence, the professional acumen of the 'stars' was questionable. Before the monopoly of the Imperial theatres was abolished in 1882, actor-coaching was rare. Even when training programmes did become established, 'many actresses and actors firmly rejected the idea that acting was a learned skill' (ibid.: 39). So how did young actors acquire their craft? By imitating the great performers, of course! Even Stanislavsky confessed that his usual practice as an amateur was to copy blindly his favourite artist of the Imperial Maly Theatre. He memorised every bit of business in the great actor's interpretation of a role, learning the full range of his gestures and intonations, and leaving Stanislavsky's own directors with nothing to do. After all, he had already 'acquired' his performance, albeit second-hand. But how else could young actors learn when there was no written 'manual' that might help them? Thus, a type of performance evolved in which shouting, exaggerated gestures and simple characterisations were all 'larded with animal temperament' — and that was considered 'full-toned acting' (Stanislavsky 1984: 40). The artistic climate into which Stanislavsky emerged as a theatre practitioner was fairly bleak: a chaos devoid of coherent stage pictures, design concepts, directorial decisions, trained professionals and ensemble companies. Under these conditions, and without an acting 'A–Z', Stanislavsky began his process of 'revolution'.

THE THEATRICAL REVOLUTION

Stanislavsky's theatrical revolution began in earnest with his famously long conversation with Vladimir Nemirovich-Danchenko on 22 June 1897. Nemirovich was an award-winning playwright and teacher at the Philharmonic School and, on his instigation, the two men met at the stylish Moscow haunt, the Slavyansky Bazaar. Having been struck by

Stanislavsky's acting, and knowing of the family's wealth, Nemirovich invited him to discuss the prospects of founding a new theatre. His intention was to harness the talent of his own pupils with Stanislavsky's amateur colleagues; at the same time, he couldn't disguise the fact that he had an eye on those Alekseyev roubles. . . . The meeting lasted from 2 p.m. until 8 a.m. the following morning, during which time the two men heatedly debated artistic ideals, staging techniques, discipline and ethics, organisational strategies, future repertoire and their respective responsibilities. The only major hiccup was Stanislavsky's refusal to jeopardise his family's fortune. Nonetheless, the pioneering discussion forged an alliance and, by the summer of the following year, the first season of the fledgling Moscow Art Theatre was deep in rehearsal, with Stanislavsky serving as an actor and director.

His main artistic concern was that the new company should explode the emptiness of traditional theatre practice; instead, plays should be infused with psychological content. The troublesome question was whose task was it to create that psychological content: the actors or the directors? Knowing no better, Stanislavsky began with the Director.

THE DIRECTOR DICTATOR: 1891–1906

WHERE THE IDEAS CAME FROM

Stanislavsky's directing strategy involved a 'production plan', which he created by filling a playtext with a myriad of details that he thought out before rehearsals began. The details concerned every aspect of the play: how to move, how to act, where and when to change positions (a little like working out the 'blocking'), even the kind of voices that he thought the actors should use. Once the production plan was prepared, the actors then had to carry out his directions with total and unquestioning precision.

The summer of 1898 wasn't the first time Stanislavsky had used a production plan. He had in fact developed this practice out of two formative encounters with professional directors in his early career. The first of these was Fedotov of the Society of Art and Literature, whose directing style had revealed to Stanislavsky the value of preparing a careful and artistic plan. It wasn't always easy, however, to convert the plan – or *mise-en-scène* – into actual stage pictures. Fedotov often resorted to demonstrating for his actors the style or the physicality that he wanted them to use. The trouble was that their performances often consisted of nothing more than poor imitations of his exciting demonstrations. (Stanislavsky himself had fallen victim to this with his Miserly Knight in 1888.) A second major influence on Stanislavsky's directing style emerged in 1890, when the German Saxe-Meiningen players performed in Russia. Their director, Ludwig Chronegk, choreographed the company with a discipline so military that vast and dynamic crowd scenes could be incorporated into his productions. Stanislavsky was extremely impressed with the ensemble effects, as well as the details of lighting, scenery, costume and sound. It was the first time that he had seen authentic-looking sets and heard made-to-order soundscapes, and he was so bowled over that he attended all the performances, devoting an entire album to careful notes and drawings of each play.

With a combination of Chronegk's autocratic discipline and Fedotov's understanding of the 'blocking', or *mise-en-scène*, Stanislavsky began his first directing job for the Society of Art and Literature in 1891 with *The Fruits of Enlightenment* by Lev Tolstoy (1828–1910). By 1898, when the infant Moscow Art Theatre staged *The Seagull* in its opening season, Stanislavsky had had seven years to establish his particular directing style, which toppled dangerously towards dictatorship.

PUTTING IT INTO PRACTICE

Although the history of *The Seagull* by Anton Chekhov (1860–1904) is discussed in greater detail in Chapter 3, there are a number of important points to be raised here. *The Seagull* was unlike anything seen on the stage before. There were no traditional character 'types', nor any recognisable structural devices, such as exposition (the unravelling of the plot) and dénouement (the revelatory climax). Instead, Chekhov introduced 'inner **activity**' to the dramatic form, full of nuances and suggestions. These innovations were exceptionally challenging to actors and audience alike. In fact, the play's 1896 premiere at the Aleksandrinsky Theatre in St Petersburg was a legendary 'failure'. Without the familiar conventions and formulae, the acting company floundered. Chekhov himself could hardly help: he was neither an actor nor a director and had no means of alerting them to the delicate style of playing. Robbed of their usual *emplois* (types), the actors had nothing to sustain them.

Enter Stanislavsky, two years later, to rise to the challenge with the Moscow Art Theatre. He immediately put his directing method into practice. Hiding in a study in the Ukraine, he beavered away diligently from 12 August until 20 September 1898 to construct the production plans. They included extensive character notes and detailed staging, from the barking of dogs to the croaking of frogs to create a realistic atmosphere. Although Stanislavsky didn't understand the play, the imaginative details of his *mises-en-scène* somehow unlocked the difficulties of Chekhov's psychological writing in a way that the Aleksandrinsky company had previously failed to do. As the plan of each act was completed, Stanislavsky sent the notes to Pushkino near Moscow, where Nemirovich-Danchenko rehearsed them with the newly formed acting company. The relay between Stanislavsky and Nemirovich was by no means satisfactory: it meant that Chekhov's intentions were filtered through two directors before the actors' interpretation was even considered. Not that it would have made much difference: Stanislavsky had yet to appreciate the personal contribution that actors themselves could make. Nonetheless, his choices as a director were so evocative that Chekhov honoured the production plans as 'amazing, the like of which have never been seen in Russia' (cited in Benedetti 1990: 79).

THE PITFALLS OF THE *MISE-EN-SCÈNE*

Stanislavsky's success in creating the *mises-en-scène* lay in his ability to turn the nuances of Chekhov's script into very specific directions for the actors. Unfortunately, the details that worked on paper in the Ukraine didn't always translate smoothly to the rehearsal room in Pushkino. Part of the problem was that, whether he knew it or not, Stanislavsky was setting in motion two revolutions at the same time. The first revolution concerned *theatre production* and the actual attention to detail on stage, and the second revolution focused on *acting styles* and the 'truthful' portrayal of what he called the **life of the human spirit** (Stanislavsky 1984: 171). In the summer of 1898, he possessed the tools with which to tackle only the first (the external form) and not the second (the inner content). Without addressing form and content together, he was in danger of exchanging one convention – demonstrational acting – for another convention – Naturalism.

Naturalism was introduced to the international literary scene in 1868 by the French writer, Émile Zola (1840–1902). The preoccupation of the Naturalists was to investigate 'man' as a product of his heredity (his genes) and his environment (his upbringing): are we simply born the way we are or can we do something about it? To examine this essentially scientific theory, Zola recreated in his novels a 'slice of life' – an imitation of the real world; a fictional 'crucible' in which human behaviour could be analysed and dissected.

Stanislavsky was clearly intrigued by the imitation of real life as his *Seagull* production plan illustrates (see Chapter 3). However, he was so insistent on naturalistic detail that Chekhov's initial thrill with the production plan was completely wiped out. He grew incensed at the pedantic 'truth' that Stanislavsky demanded of the actors – 'But the theatre is art! . . . You forget, you don't have a fourth wall!' (Chekhov cited in Melchinger 1972: 4).

In Stanislavsky's defence, he struggled hard to penetrate the complex writing of Chekhov, whose new dramatic form was steeped in contradictions. The idiosyncrasies of the characters couldn't always be formulated intellectually on the pages of a production plan: they required the breath of the live actors. Yet they were caught in a 'catch-22': the script needed the actors' psychological-physical selves, but they had no psychological-physical vocabulary. At this stage in his career, Stanislavsky was really none the wiser, and all he could do was resort to the same level of whip-cracking that he had used with the Society of Art and Literature. He later confessed that:

I was helped by the despotism I had learned from Chronegk. I demanded obedience and I got it . . . I cared little for the inner emotions of the actor. I sincerely thought it was possible to order others to live and feel according to another's will. I gave orders to all and for all places of the performance and these orders were binding for all.

(Stanislavsky 1984: 41, 43)

THE SUBJUGATION OF THE ACTORS

Of course it was impossible to 'order others to live and feel according to another's will', and the Art Theatre actors were adrift in the whole process. They needed guidance as to how they might flood the externally-imposed actions with their own inner life, but their director couldn't give it. They were utterly frustrated. After all, the Moscow Art Theatre had been founded to revolutionise all aspects of the theatre, and yet here was Stanislavsky, blatantly denying one of its crucial components – the acting ensemble – its own creative freedom. As Vsevolod Meyerhold (1874–1940), one of its dynamic young actors, complained:

> Are we the cast really supposed to do *nothing but* act? We also want to *think* while we're acting. We want to know *why* we are acting, *what* we are acting and who we are teaching or criticizing by our acting.
>
> (cited in Benedetti 1991: 45)

Despite the cast's complaints, Stanislavsky persisted with his autocratic directing for all of Chekhov's successive works: *Uncle Vanya* (1899), *Three Sisters* (1901) and *The Cherry Orchard* (1903). His insistence that they accept his production plans continued to cause grief among his actors, who felt robbed of their potential input. Working on *Uncle Vanya*, Olga Knipper (1868–1959), one of the Art Theatre's founder members and Chekhov's wife, was obliged to abandon her own characterisation of Elena before she had had the chance to develop it properly. Stanislavsky found her interpretation 'boring', and insisted that she adopt *his* concept instead, saying it was 'essential for the play'. Knipper wrote to Chekhov, declaring that it was 'awful to think of the future, of the work ahead, if I have to resist the director's yoke again' (cited in Benedetti 1991: 65). New rehearsal methods were becoming a matter of artistic urgency.

A TASTE OF HIS OWN MEDICINE

By 1902 – scarcely four years into its existence – the Moscow Art Theatre faced a potential crisis. It was widely accused of being too naturalistic, and disagreements between Stanislavsky and Nemirovich-Danchenko over creative style had grown acute. Added to this, the

Figure 1.3 Stanislavsky as Satin in Gorky's *The Lower Depths* (1903)

ensemble was disrupted when the valued actor, Meyerhold, was deliberately omitted from the list of Art Theatre shareholders. He quit
the company, taking with him a number of angry allies. There was a
general state of artistic and internal turmoil. Stanislavsky's faith in his
own acting was cracking, and a series of collisions with Nemirovich-
Danchenko fuelled his crisis of confidence. Referring to his interpretation of Satin in *The Lower Depths* (1902) by Maksim Gorky (1868–
1936), Nemirovich declared that Stanislavsky needed a new method of
acting. He had worn out his old method, and it was time to show
himself 'to be a different performer from the one that the Art Theatre
had come to know' (Nemirovich-Danchenko cited in Benedetti 1991:
140) (see Figure 1.3).

Stanislavsky's personal dissatisfaction was exacerbated in 1903. He
was working with Nemirovich on the role of Brutus in Shakespeare's

Julius Caesar, during which time, Nemirovich was evolving his own theory of the 'creative producer'. As the director of *Julius Caesar*, Nemirovich adopted a stance that was startlingly reminiscent of Stanislavsky's own dictatorial intransigence:

> My production plan is a complete treatise. . . . I have prepared everything . . . with great care and intend to dragoon the cast into what I have written with conviction. . . . I see the tone and tempo of the second act, especially for Brutus, *absolutely* differently from you. . . . And I intend to follow my line without restraint.
>
> (Nemirovich-Danchenko cited in Benedetti 1991: 155)

Stanislavsky felt straitjacketed by Nemirovich's direction, and suddenly he realised the fundamental problem with the production-plan technique. Because the ideas in the *mise-en-scène* were not the actors' own, but were forced upon them by the director, they struggled to find their own *inner justification* for their on-stage actions. Without a real sense of inner justification, the *mise-en-scène* – however imaginative – was no more 'truthful' than the clichéd, representational acting from which Stanislavsky wanted to break. Once he understood this, he realised that supreme power had to be taken from the director. His unsettling experience on *Julius Caesar* convinced him that the production-plan technique was 'despotic'. Now he sought new strategies, in which directors studied their actors beforehand and depended on their contribution in rehearsal. That didn't mean that detailed research into the playscript wasn't essential. It was simply a question of how and by whom this work should be done. In his search to create the 'life of the human spirit', Stanislavsky turned his attention away from the *director's* interpretation of a play to the *company's* creative contributions.

ROUND-THE-TABLE ANALYSIS: 1906– EARLY 1930s

WHAT WAS IT AND WHY DO IT?

It was time to give the actors some power. Stanislavsky threw away the notion that he should devise the *mise-en-scène* on his own; instead, he gathered the acting company around the table, where together they unravelled a playtext and its characters. Their detective work took a variety of forms: they retold the content of the play, and made lists of all the facts, events, and **given circumstances** proposed by the play-wright. They thought up questions and provided the answers. They studied the words and **pauses** between them. They invented past and future lives for the characters. They analysed the play's structure, breaking it into sections – or **bits** – and finding names for the char-acters' **objectives** – or 'tasks'. There were discussions and debates, which sometimes focused on spatial relationships, sometimes on psychological motivations. All these differing practical methods were 'part of the single process of analysis, or coming to know the play and your parts' (Stanislavsky 2000b: 155).

The aim of Stanislavsky's round-the-table analysis was very specific: through discussing the play, the company could feel that they 'owned' the production, that they all had responsibility for the creation of their characters and atmospheres. So discussions weren't head-bound and intellectual, but imaginative and even emotional. Harnessing emotions was a key concern for Stanislavsky during this stage of his professional evolution. Thus, he developed the concept of 'affective memory', a term adopted from the French psychologist, Théodule Ribot (1839–1916). At its most simplistic, the sequence behind affective memory (or 'emotion memory') was easy: actors began by remembering from their own life an experience that was analogous to an event in the play. They then conjured up memories of all the physical and sensory details that were originally connected with that personal experience. Once these memories were sufficiently powerful, the actors related them to the given circumstances of their *characters'* situations, so that the fictional roles could be flooded with real emotional content. (Stanislavsky had hoped that this would happen with the night in the cellar and the Miserly Knight!)

The combination of imagination, emotional recollection and textual analysis certainly fuelled Stanislavsky's rehearsal practices in the early 1900s. With his growing need to identify the tangible means of bringing to the stage 'the life of the human spirit', his round-the-table discussions extended from several hours to several months, as the actors became more and more involved.

ASSAILING ACTOR-TRAINING THROUGH THE THEATRICAL STUDIO

If his actors were to become increasingly involved in the creative process, the very foundations of *actor-training* would have to be reconsidered. It was all well and good experimenting in the rehearsal room, but what if the actors' basic tools were rusty, or even dormant? Stanislavsky knew that he had to go right in at ground level – via the classroom. The attachment of a drama school to the Moscow Art Theatre had always been a significant part of Stanislavsky and Nemirovich's plans and, from the moment the Theatre was founded, ongoing classes were an accepted part of the timetable. However, the acting disciplines at the Theatre's school as it existed in 1902 were fairly traditional, with classes in diction, declamation, singing, recitation, dance and juggling. What was needed was an entirely new technique, in which the actors' inner life was also considered.

Stanislavsky's fascination with 'inner life' may well have been sparked by a critical article entitled 'Unnecessary Truth', written in 1902 by Valery Bryusov (1873–1924), one of the leading exponents of the Russian Symbolist movement. For Bryusov, theatre and the *art of the actor* were the same thing: one couldn't exist without the other. Clearly this article rattled Stanislavsky's cage, but it wasn't the only provocation. During the 1904–5 season at the Moscow Art Theatre, he decided to stage three plays by the Belgian playwright, Maurice Maeterlinck (1862–1949). The content of these symbolist dramas soon highlighted – even more than the naturalistic texts – that the live contribution of the performers was vital for exploring their ethereal, 'spiritual' quality. Unfortunately, his actors just weren't equipped to

---

Symbolism thrived in the first two decades of the twentieth century. At its heart lay the desire to transcend the crude realities of everyday life that the Naturalist movement strove to imitate. Instead, the Symbolists explored the way in which supernatural and mystical reverberations impacted on man's existence. Bryusov's article attacked naturalistic detail, arguing that the only 'real' thing on the stage was the actor's physical body.

balance the technical demands of performance with the esoteric content of the plays.

How then was Stanislavsky to train them? He understood through his work on the Symbolist plays that acting was a 'two-way street': inner life couldn't exist without the human 'casing' of a physical body, yet the outmoded representational school of acting had proved that physicality alone was shallow and boring without the actors' 'inner' connection. Stanislavsky recognised Bryusov's declaration that theatre was a *physical* medium; at the same time, he saw that his actors' bodies were fairly limited compared with ballet dancers or gymnasts. He was in another 'catch-22': he yearned for physically versatile performers, yet he had no means of training them. To help him in his dilemma, he turned to the 'new ways' that were being explored by former company member, Vsevelod Meyerhold. Meyerhold hungered for a performance medium that was physical, political and unshamedly theatrical. In response to the potential of Meyerhold's dynamic techniques, Stanislavsky set up an offshoot of the Moscow Art Theatre in 1905, and they called it the Theatrical Studio.

The Theatrical Studio proved to be Stanislavsky's first concrete step towards developing a psycho-physical training ground in which the actors' psychology and physicality were equally important. It was 'neither a ready-made theatre nor a school for beginners, but a laboratory for more or less mature actors' (Stanislavsky 1982: 430). Stanislavsky was to fund it, while Meyerhold, whom he invited back into the fold after three years' absence, was given artistic and pedagogical freedom. The techniques proposed by Meyerhold in the Theatrical Studio were truly progressive. He abandoned discussion and focused on improvisation. (In many ways, his practices were precursors of those adopted by Stanislavsky almost thirty years later with his **Method of Physical Actions**.) Yet it quickly transpired with Meyerhold's production of Maeterlinck's *The Death of Tintagiles* that the Theatrical Studio was trying to run before it could walk. There was still no specific vocabulary with which to tackle an acting revolution. Neither Meyerhold's Biomechanics (a precise form of acrobatic-based training) nor Stanislavsky's 'system' had yet been formulated. Added to which there was an inherent contradiction between Stanislavsky's artistic ambitions and those held by Meyerhold. Meyerhold pursued the path of *physical* theatre, in which there was little room for psychology or emotion. Stanislavsky, on the other hand, was striving for a *psycho-*

physical theatre, where gesture was invested with *emotional* content, as well as theatrical expression. And so, in spite of – or perhaps because of – Meyerhold's innovative ideas, the Theatrical Studio closed after only five months. The political upheaval caused by the first Russian Revolution in 1905 might have been partially responsible for the Studio's demise. Unfortunately, it doesn't dispel the unavoidable dichotomy that existed between the two directors' idealistic visions and the reality of their pursuits. Nonetheless, the role of the Theatrical Studio as a pioneering forum for testing some kind of psycho-physicality shouldn't be underestimated.

THE HOLIDAY IN FINLAND

The following year – 1906 – proved to be a critical one in terms of the development of Stanislavsky's 'system'. The closure of the Theatrical Studio, along with Chekhov's death, the failure of the Symbolist plays, a dissatisfaction with the artistic ethos of the Moscow Art Theatre, political and social unrest throughout Russia, financial disaster and a growing despair with the inadequacies of his own craft forced Stanislavsky to reassess the basic mechanics of acting. His relationship with Nemirovich-Danchenko had been deteriorating for several years, and at various times both parties had threatened to quit the company. The cause of the disputes was complex, but at the heart of it lay the fact that Nemirovich was a *writer* and a *director*: the text and the final production were for him the critical elements. Stanislavsky, on the other hand, was an investigator, an experimenter, as well as a director. He now believed that the *actor* was at the heart of the performance and, at this stage in his artistic credo, he didn't revere the writer. (He had even suggested during their 1904 production of *Ghosts* by the realist dramatist, Henrik Ibsen (1828–1906), that he rewrite the opening lines, as the text didn't fit his **physical actions**.) It was, therefore, extremely depressing when, in 1906, while touring with the Art Theatre in Europe, Stanislavsky found that his own acting had become mechanical and empty. In a state of personal unrest, he took his family on a much-needed holiday to Finland. Once there, he hid away in a darkened room, smoked endlessly and surrounded himself with twenty years of notebooks, each filled with his scribblings on acting, rehearsing and directing. He began a complicated and soul-searching attempt to organise formally a practical acting 'system'.

Stanislavsky believed that his evolving 'system' was essentially a means of applying natural and biological laws to the conventions of the theatre. He took as his starting point moments in his own stage experiences and his observations of famous actors, when spontaneity seemed to take over and 'the life of the human spirit' appeared on the stage. He then tried to isolate those moments, analyse them and put them back together in a formalised way *via* his 'system', so that all actors at any time could tap into their own spontaneous inspiration. The 'system' had two distinct but parallel branches: (1) practical exercises to develop the actor's physical, vocal and emotional instrument (Actor-Training or *the work on the self*); and (2) cerebral methods of round-the-table analysis to explode the hidden mysteries of a playtext (Rehearsal Techniques or *the work on the role*).

The *work on the self* also had two prongs – inner and outer. In the course of time, Stanislavsky developed exercises to help inner preparation through meditation, relaxation, concentration and imagination. Inner work was paralleled with the outer preparation of the actor's raw materials. Those raw materials included a strong voice, perfect diction, plasticity of movement, a characterful face and expressive hands, a vivid imagination and 'an infectious stage charm' (Stanislavsky cited in Gorchakov 1991: 193–4). Because these tools were in a continual state of development, Stanislavsky maintained that actors should complement their stage work with lifelong training to accommodate those changes.

Work on the role consisted of round-the-table analysis, as well as entering into the character's psychology through historical research, imagination and affective memory. Stanislavsky's intention was that the 'bi-focal' preparation of the self and the role would help actors to dive into a 'creative state'. The 'creative state' was one in which they felt so physically, mentally and emotionally open that they could stimulate their 'creative will'. The 'creative will' was the dynamo for acting in a spontaneous, exciting and unexpected way.

THE DRAMA OF LIFE AND A MONTH IN THE COUNTRY

Following the fruitful holiday in Finland, Stanislavsky used the various studios that emerged alongside the Moscow Art Theatre's main house in the years between 1905 and 1927 as 'laboratories'. In these 'laboratories', he explored different genres of play, trying out numerous experiments to combine the two aspects of his 'system': Actor-Training and Rehearsal Techniques. The most significant 'laboratory' was arguably the First Studio, formed in 1912 and devoted to theatrical adventures involving the genius actor, Mikhail Chekhov (1891–1955), the pioneering director, Evgeny Vakhtangov (1883–1923), and the inspirational teacher, Leopold Sulerzhitsky (1872–1916). Prior to this, productions in the Moscow Art Theatre's main house were also used to experiment and test out various rehearsal techniques. Two of the most challenging of these were the allegorical *The Drama of Life* (1907) by Nobel prize-winning Norwegian author, Knut Hamsun (1859–1952), and the more naturalistic drama, *A Month in the Country* (1909), by Ivan Turgenev (1818–83). In both productions, Stanislavsky served as director, as well as taking the role of Kareno in the first and Ratikin in the second (see Figure 1.4).

The Drama of Life was the first production in which Stanislavsky consciously examined 'the *inner character* of the play and its roles' (Stanislavsky 1982: 474). The 'system' was still in its embryonic state, and he lacked the tools to execute this work succinctly and effectively. Nonetheless, the particular experiment that he undertook in rehearsals focused on intangible levels of communication, that he called 'irradiation' or **communion**. 'Communion' was a concept stemming from the Eastern meditational practices of his inspiring colleague, Leopold Sulerzhitsky. 'Suler' was first introduced to the Moscow Art Theatre in 1903, and by 1906 he had become an assistant director and teacher, despite the fact that Nemirovich was suspicious of his influence and refused to acknowledge him officially as a member of staff. With an eclectic past as a singer, a trained artist, a fisherman in the Crimea, scholar, shepherd and sailor, Suler's most profound contribution to Stanislavsky's development was his introduction of Hatha yoga into the actor-training programme.

Hatha yoga dates back more than 5,000 years, the word 'yoga' meaning 'union, to join or yoke together'. The basic principle of Hatha yoga is that exercise (asana) combines with breathing (pranayama) to relax the body and integrate the mind and emotions. It is clear to see why Stanislavsky considered yoga to be a vital part of actor-training.

Suler's influence on the experiments with *The Drama of Life* is evident, especially with one exercise involving complete immobility. During this particular exercise, Stanislavsky forbade his actors to use any external means of presenting a character – neither gesture nor movement. Instead he wanted:

> bodiless passion in its pure, naked form, both naturally and emanating directly from the soul of the actor. For the transmission of this . . . the artist needed only eyes, face and mime. So let him, in immobility, live through the emotion he has to transmit with the help of feeling and temperament.
>
> (cited in Worrall 1996: 173)

Through the 'immobility' exercise, Stanislavsky wanted his actors to realise how powerful stillness and silence could be. He also wanted them to feel the resonances of their own emotional repertoires and the wealth of information that they could glean from each other just by allowing the space between them to be 'alive'. (See Chapter 2 for details of 'communion' and Chapter 4 for exercises.)

Two years later – in 1909 – Stanislavsky's rehearsals for *A Month in the Country* involved an even stranger new practice. Up until now, he had adopted a predominantly cerebral approach, either through production plans (such as *The Seagull*) or round-the-table discussions. However, the more he experimented with psycho-physical exercises involving the actors' bodies and imaginations, the more he questioned intellectual activities. Not quite daring to let go completely of the brain-based preparatory work, Stanislavsky came up with a bizarre and potentially compromised blend of analysis and spirituality for *A Month in the Country*. As usual, the first rehearsals took place round the table. Rather than embarking on discussions of context or dramatic structure, Stanislavsky began to dictate, and the actors carefully noted down, 'the symbolic designations of the various emotions and inner states' suggested by the text (Koonen cited in Worrall 1996: 186). These 'symbolic designations' ranged from a question mark indicating 'surprise', or a question mark in brackets indicating 'hidden surprise', to a large dash denoting 'stage apathy', a cross denoting 'the creative state' and an upward-pointing arrow denoting 'the transition from apathy to the creative state'. The hieroglyphics littered the text to signpost the characters' emotional journeys, which the actors were then expected to experience. This was all very strange: to ask the actors

Figure 1.4 Stanislavsky as Ratikin in Turgenev's *A Month in the Country* (1909)

to embody big emotional transitions at the points the director indicated was far more complex than Stanislavsky's former insistence on detailed, naturalistic *mises-en-scène*. As actress, Alisa Koonen (1889–1974), declared: 'The exercises associated with the "system" turned out to be difficult all round. What was demanded was not simply the mechanical execution of the task, but also our inner participation' (cited in Worrall 1996: 186).

To some extent, Stanislavsky's bizarre exercises in immobility and hieroglyphics go to show that he knew that he was on to something exciting with the idea of 'inner life' and 'creative state'; he simply didn't know how to access them formally. There was a danger that the hieroglyphics were just another form of artistic straitjacketing, no better than a production plan. By 1910, however, Stanislavsky's rehearsal methods had been simplified: the actors were now asked to identify the rather more attainable 'bits' of a text (often translated as 'units') and 'tasks' of a character (often translated as 'objectives'). This process combined and activated what Stanislavsky called the three **inner motive forces** of thought, will and emotion. Through intellectual analysis (via the thought-centre), the actors determined what they were *doing* (in the action- or will-centre) and why they *wanted* to do it (through the emotion- or feeling-centre).

By 1910, the major components of bits, tasks, affective memory, inner motive forces and communion had been identified. Stanislavsky's 'system' was in place. (See Chapter 2 for details of all these terms.)

THE STATE OF 'I AM'

For more than ten years, Stanislavsky continued to refine his 'system', supplementing his practical experiments by delving into books on psychology and philosophy. During this period, the double-pronged training of 'work on the self' and 'work on the role' led Stanislavsky to adjust his definition of what he had previously called 'personality' acting. He had come to believe that actors could only work from their own raw materials if they really wanted to stir their creative wills. In other words, they had to put themselves into the characters' circumstances and ask themselves: 'What would *I* do in this situation? What do I *want*? Where am I *going*?' By stimulating these questions, the actors' personalities were directly linked to the circumstances of the play.

There was a significant difference between this new kind of 'personality acting' and the kind for which Stanislavsky had yearned in his vainglorious, swashbuckling youth as the Miserly Knight. Although actors might now *begin* with their own personality, they didn't stop there: they stepped *beyond* their individual *emplois* into the character as written by the playwright. This transition provoked many questions for Stanislavsky about the relationship between actor and role and, in 1914, he altered his notion of the 'creative state' to the state of 'I am': 'I am in this situation (albeit imaginary), so I will respond as truthfully as I can for the character'. Quite possibly it was drastic international events as much as personal artistic probings that caused this change in his terminology. In 1914, the year in which the First World War broke out, Stanislavsky found himself caught in the Swiss frontier town of Immerstadt while travelling with some of his family and colleagues. Having been dragged from a train, accused of being a Russian spy and threatened with death at gunpoint, it is hardly surprising that his mind had turned to questions of existence and ideas of who 'I am'.

Some years later, in 1923–4, the Moscow Art Theatre embarked on two tours of America to ease the Theatre's ailing finances. The Americans had gone wild for the Russian 'psychological' acting, and were hungry for lectures and lessons to help them achieve equally detailed performances themselves. By 1924, Stanislavsky provided an actual step-by-step guide into the state of 'I am', beginning with factual knowledge and ending with heartfelt emotion. At the centre of this 'guide' lay the actors' need to search for the 'right bait' – that is, the right **actions** – to arouse their feeling. Having 'caught the feeling', actors had to learn how to control it. Inspirational acting depended upon a fine balance between conscious control and subconscious spontaneity. (The fact that Stanislavsky placed 'actions' at the heart of the fourth stage signals that he was already moving towards the Method of Physical Actions and **Active Analysis**.)

DEAD SOULS – A TURNING POINT

Stanislavsky's ideas never remained static for very long, which was why he considered that his 'system' wasn't a gospel but simply a tool to assist actors when they had trouble with a role. The unexpected announcement by Nemirovich-Danchenko in 1911 that the 'system' was to be adopted by all the Moscow Art Theatre practitioners didn't

Nikolai Gogol (1809–52) was a playwright of extraordinary comic genius, who combined grotesque physicality with realistic psychology, his most celebrated drama being *The Inspector General* (1836).

please him one jot! Even less satisfactory was Stalin's own formalisation of the 'system' in 1934. This formalisation totally contradicted Stanislavsky's own belief that 'Nothing can be more harmful to art than the use of a method for its own sake' (1990: 142). Added to this, Stanislavsky was always experimenting, therefore always moving on. How could his 'theories' be set in stone? In fact, after years of variations on round-the-table research, he came to the conclusion in 1932 that analysis could be limiting. The production that brought Stanislavsky to this conclusion was Nikolai Gogol's *Dead Souls* (1846).

Four years before *Dead Souls*, in 1928, Stanislavsky had suffered a heart attack on stage during a gala performance to celebrate the Art Theatre's thirtieth anniversary. As a result, he had retired from acting, and now devoted his time to teaching and directing. To prepare for *Dead Souls*, his cast embarked on extensive research into Gogol's letters, biography, works and portraiture. One of the leading actors, Vasily Toporkov (1889–1970), grumbled that, while they all found the visits to museums and galleries fascinating and the discussions stimulating, they couldn't translate their intellectual investigations into anything useful on stage. Toporkov wasn't the only one to question the rehearsal methods. Another very experienced actress had serious problems. She was Stanislavsky's wife, Lilina, who had been with the Moscow Art Theatre since its foundation. For some reason, during the rehearsals of *Dead Souls*, she seemed to abandon all her intuition, embarking instead upon 'a painstaking, corroding analysis, with unnecessary reflection and excessive self-control'. Stanislavsky's advice to her was wonderfully reassuring, declaring that: 'It is not necessary for you to understand everything in the scene. Meticulousness can be a plague for the actor; he starts to split hairs, [and] place a mass of unnecessary details between himself and his partner' (cited in Toporkov 1998: 133). Obviously, Stanislavsky had become as wary of extensive round-the-table analysis as he was of his former directorial autocracy. He now rejected the practice of telling actors to:

'Go on stage, perform your roles and apply what you have learned during the past few months of work around the table.' With a swollen head and empty heart, the actors go on stage and are unable to play anything at all. They need many more months in order to discard the superfluous, to select and assimilate the necessary, in order to find themselves – even at moments – in the new role.

(Stanislavsky cited in Moore 1973: 31)

The experience of *Dead Souls* had taught Stanislavsky that actors have to 'let go of their homework'. That wasn't to say that they shouldn't do the preparation in the first place, but, just as a pianist stops thinking about digital dexterity when playing a concerto, so too should actors 'forget' their preparation at the point when it has served its purpose. Accurate research was no longer as interesting to Stanislavsky as unexpected interpretations and the possibility of inspiration.

How then might actors experience artistic inspiration? By now Stanislavsky knew that the answer lay in *action*: finding the right action was the challenge to which he turned his attention in his final voyage of discovery.

THE FINAL LEGACIES: 1930s–1938 AND BEYOND

THE OPERA-DRAMATIC STUDIO

At the age of seventy-three, Stanislavsky knew that the only way he could conduct his final experimentations was away from the main house of the Moscow Art Theatre. By the 1930s, the Art Theatre had long ago ceased to be a hotbed of theatrical innovation. Since it had been declared a paradigm of cultural heritage in 1917, it had become little more than a museum shackled to Socialist rule. Therefore, in 1935, Stanislavsky and his sister, Zinaïda, drew together a circle of young and talented protégés to open his last 'satellite laboratory' – the Opera-Dramatic Studio. It was situated in his own apartment on 6, Leontievski Lane in Moscow, and here he remained locked away for the rest of his life.

Politically, Stanislavsky was well informed, but naive: although he read the written words of the newspaper, he had a peculiar ignorance – or blindness – to their subtext and undercurrents. As he grew older

Joseph Stalin was elected general secretary of the Communist Party in 1922, from which position he defeated all major opponents, so that, five years after the death of Soviet leader, Lenin, in 1924, Stalin was in the position to become dictator of the USSR. His absolute – autocratic and cruel – Socialist power went unchallenged until his death from a stroke in 1953.

and sicker, and immersed himself deeper in his practical research, he was oblivious to the fact that he was essentially under house arrest. He was, in the words of Joseph Stalin (1879–1953), 'isolated, but preserved'. All Stanislavsky's meetings were surreptitiously controlled by his doctors who themselves were under the strictest orders 'from above'. In secluded ignorance, Stanislavsky focused the Opera-Dramatic Studio on the process of training and rehearsal, without worrying about the results of a full-scale production.

THE METHOD OF PHYSICAL ACTIONS

How it came about

Stanislavsky's lifelong search was for a rehearsal technique that would engage body, mind and emotions simultaneously. His youthful experiments had led him to predetermine a *mise-en-scène* and then analytically research a text. But, by 1935, he seriously questioned whether either of those rehearsal methods was any good in terms of its psycho-physical possibilities. His work in the early 1900s had convinced Stanislavsky that real human feelings were a vital part of good acting, and that every gifted performer possessed the appropriate raw materials. It was just a matter of finding the 'right bait' to arouse them. Over the years, he had tried to find the 'right bait' through analysis, observation, affective memory and imagination. The tricky part was that, once actors' emotions were aroused, they had to be able to stop them in an instant, and to change them as appropriate. Yet Stanislavsky recognised that the emotion-centre was highly capricious and, as such, almost impossible to manipulate consciously. The fascinating contradiction in the acting process, therefore, was how to arouse and then control something as teasingly uncontrollable as emotion.

Stanislavsky's career had been devoted to unravelling this troublesome contradiction, and by the end of his life, he believed that he had discovered a possible solution to the emotion/experience dichotomy. Instead of true emotion being the *end*-product of an acting technique, he wanted to devise a rehearsal process of which emotion was a *by*-product. In other words, he sought a process in which emotions arose inevitably from the actions, rather than actors consciously trying to arouse emotions as the main challenge to their acting skills. After all, the emotion-centre wasn't the only piece in the jigsaw: an actor's intricate mechanism also included the other two 'inner motive forces' of will and thought. Could it be that, if actors actively *did* something (will) and fully *believed* in what they were doing (thought), appropriate emotions might arise accordingly?

Action! Action! Action! became the focal point of Stanislavsky's new technique and, in 1935, he addressed his Opera students, proclaiming that: 'now we shall proceed differently. We shall create the line of physical action' (cited in Magarshack 1950: 389). That was the crux of it: *the line of physical action*, and the shift of emphasis from inner emotion to on-stage action was described by his young actor Toporkov as 'one of Stanislavski's greatest discoveries' (1998: 58).

'Physical actions' were small, achievable tasks that were directed straight towards the other actors on stage; the motives behind those actions were both practical and psychological. To illustrate what he meant, Stanislavsky took the example of the highly dramatic situation of the jealous composer, Salieri, plotting the murder of his arch-rival, Mozart. Salieri manages to poison Mozart by means of a series of simple physical actions: 'first by choosing a wine glass, next by pouring the wine, next by dropping in the poison, and only then by handing the glass to his rival' (Stanislavsky cited in Carnicke in Hodge 2000: 26). Through this kind of logical progression, actors found that small, achievable tasks could encapsulate great psychological complexities. So these actions weren't an end in themselves, but rather they propelled the actor into 'complex psychological emotional experiences' (Chushkin in Foreword to Toporkov 1998: 17). At the same time, they were so simple and direct that actors could accomplish them without any emotional strain whatsoever.

Rehearsal technique: finding the 'score of physical actions'

The main purpose of the Method of Physical Actions was for actors to find the precise and logical sequence of actions that would enable their characters to achieve their 'tasks'. The technique for doing this was in fact very simple, and Stanislavsky's challenge to his company was provocative: 'Without any reading, without any conferences on the play, the actors are asked to come to a rehearsal of it' (2000b: 213). How on earth could they do that? Well, the only way to rehearse a play with so little preparation had to be through improvisation. This wasn't a new idea: Meyerhold had used improvisations extensively in the 1905 Theatrical Studio. Now, in 1935, however, the improvisations were far from generalised or haphazard: if the actors were going to identify precise and truthful physical actions, they needed to pay as much attention to detail in their improvisations as they had done previously with their round-the-table analysis. The main difference was that they were no longer sitting at the table with their heads in their books and their pencils in their hands. They now did their research *on the stage*, looking into their own human lives for whatever information they needed to achieve their characters' 'tasks'.

To help actors find that information, Stanislavsky proposed four easy steps. Step 1 was as simple as possible: the actors read a scene. Step 2 involved a small amount of discussion to clarify what the scene was about, how it divided into 'bits' and what was its main 'action'. In Step 3, the actors got up and tried out the scene using improvisation. They often began with a *'silent étude'*, in which they worked attentively – but silently – through 'the line of physical action', testing whether the actions they had chosen during the preliminary discussion were appropriate or not. (Chapter 4 includes details of silent études.) After the étude, further discussions (Step 4) identified which moments had worked in the improvisation and which ones had fractured the logical line of physical action. Then the actors went back to Step 1. Little by little, words were introduced, starting with their own improvised text, then drawing closer and closer to the playwright's actual script. All the time, they returned to the simple, ongoing sequence of reading, discussing and improvising. Through these developing improvisations, the actors were able to fine-tune their actions and fix them to form the scene's 'skeleton', known as the 'score of physical actions'. This precise score could then be repeated until habit became easy and ease became beautiful. (Details of how to compile a score of physical actions can be found in Chapter 4.)

The 'creation of the living word'

In many ways, the 'score of physical actions' wasn't very different from the early predetermined plan of a *mise-en-scène*, except that the process of discovery was the complete opposite. Stanislavsky no longer provided a shopping list of actions as he had with *The Seagull*. Instead, the actors themselves unearthed the moments of 'truth' – in the characters and in the action – through their psycho-physical experience of *doing* the scene. Another reason for improvising was to personalise the learning of a text. Stanislavsky believed that:

> between our own words and those of another, the distance is of most immeasurable size. Our own words are the direct expression of our feelings, whereas the words of another are alien until we have made them our own, are nothing more than signs of future emotions which have not yet come to life inside us. Our own words are needed in the first phase of physical embodiment of a part because they are best able to extract from within us live feelings, which have not yet found their outward expression.
>
> (2000b: 100–1)

He even went as far as to forbid the deliberate memorising of the playwright's text. If actors depended too heavily on a script, he believed it revealed their reluctance – or inability – to embody the character's life. 'It was considered the highest achievement if an actor could reveal the scheme of a scene by means of purely physical actions or with the minimum number of words' (Toporkov 1998: 160).

Of course, the time would come when the actors needed the actual text, at which point in rehearsals Stanislavsky fed them with the writer's words from the sidelines, like a football coach. They grabbed these words hungrily as – by this stage – the author's text expressed a thought or carried out a piece of action much better than their own made-up speeches. The result of this process was a seemingly effortless passage from (1) the actors' improvised text, through (2) the director's prompting from the sidelines, to (3) the actors finally knowing the lines because they wanted those very words, rather than because they had formally memorised them. If the actors followed this sequence, their spoken text became what Stanislavsky called the 'creation of the living word' (2000b: 262). Its roots ran deep into their psyches, emerging as the only way to express what was going on inside them. The truly exciting moment for an actor was when the playwright's text became *action* in its own right, the vital tool for really articulating the character's burning desires.

The emergence of character

Because the emphasis of the early improvisations was on the actors' own words and real feelings, character was obviously not a major concern. In fact, 'character' was nothing more than the 'line of physical actions'. This in itself was joyously liberating. Because physical actions can come in an infinite variety of sequences and combinations, every actor had the potential to play a huge number of characters. Perhaps this was the greatest advantage of the Method of Physical Actions: it provided an easy means of expanding the actors' repertoires. No longer reliant on memories of previously experienced emotions, they could use physical actions to 'create experience where there [was] none to be remembered' (Mitter 1993: 20). In other words, murderous imaginings or analogous memories were no longer necessary for playing Macbeth. All the actor had to do was to establish a series of small achievable physical actions which by their very sequence revealed leadership, ambition, gullibility and the myriad of other qualities required for the part.

The Method of Physical Actions seemed to be a psycho-physical 'cure-all'. Stanislavsky summarised it as the simultaneous creativity of all the intellectual, emotional, spiritual and physical forces of human nature: 'this is not theoretical, but *practical research* for the sake of a genuine objective, which we attain through physical actions' (2000b: 239; my emphasis). Yet there was still another step to be taken. His understanding of 'practical research' would in fact fuel his ultimate experiment in acting practice, now known as Active Analysis.

ACTIVE ANALYSIS

Kedrov and Knebel

There's some debate among international scholars as to whether a difference between the Method of Physical Actions and Active Analysis actually exists, and certainly the overlaps are considerable. The confusion is due in part to the fact that Stanislavsky was very old and sick when these experiments were in full throttle. He himself wrote down very few of his findings, leaving his young actors, directors and teachers to hand down his 'lore' in his stead. Two individuals in particular were largely responsible for shaping his legacy: Mikhail Kedrov and Maria Knebel. Kedrov and Knebel were both involved in Stanislavsky's last projects, and in 1948 they became directors of the Stanislavsky Drama Theatre, the venture born out of the Opera-Dramatic Studio. Following Stanislavsky's death in 1938, Kedrov (who served as his assistant on *Tartuffe*, as well as playing the title role) pursued the idea of physical actions to extraordinary extremes. One of his students, now the celebrated Russian actor, Albert Filozov (1937–), found that Kedrov's desire for the logic of 'Action! Action! Action!' was so dogmatic, that the Method of Physical Actions had 'in effect killed Russian theatre' (Filozov cited in Merlin 2001: 158). Kedrov's call for 'Action!' was undoubtedly influenced by Socialist Realism.

The Socialist Realists declared that there was nothing about 'man' that couldn't be changed by social reform. Reason ruled: emotion was out! With this in mind, it is clear to see how the logical sequence of the Method of Physical Actions, particularly as promoted by Kedrov, fell in line with the scientific, 'provable' aspect of Socialist Realism.

Maria Knebel, on the other hand, was far more interested in Stanislavsky's idea of 'analysis through action', or Active Analysis.

Socialist Realism was a literary movement that came to prominence in 1934. Mirroring some of the elements of nineteenth-century Naturalism, it studied the behavioural patterns of human conduct. Unlike the Naturalists, however, the emphasis was now on environment, to the exclusion of heredity: in other words, we are not victims of our parentage, we can be whatever society wants us to be.

Active Analysis was exactly what it said: the actors analysed their roles actively by using their bodies, imaginations, intuition and emotions on the rehearsal-room floor. So – just like the Method of Physical Actions – the detective work on a play was carried out by the actors using their entire beings and not just their intellects. Unlike the Method of Physical Actions, the 'logic' of physical actions, the 'scoring' of a role, was no longer such a big deal. Anything provided the actors with valuable clues – the structure of a scene, the 'anatomy' of the play, the very *medium* of drama itself. So the logic of the sequence was less important than the experiential discoveries made through active research.

The rehearsal process

In spite of its apparently holistic appeal, the rehearsal technique still had to have a very clear process. In many ways, it echoes the stages of the Method of Physical Actions, and can be broken down into a fairly straightforward sequence (as Sharon M. Carnicke (Hodge 2000: 28–9) has so skilfully done).

First of all, the actors read the scene. Second, they assessed the facts of the scene. This involved asking questions such as: What is the event? What are the inciting objectives and resisting counter-objectives? What is the style of the piece? What language do the characters use in terms of images and rhythms? 'Assessing the facts' constituted a serious piece of textual analysis, also involving the discussion of 'bits' of action. This is important to remember, as otherwise it might seem as if Active Analysis was merely about getting up and improvising. The psycho-physical information that actors gleaned from experiencing the scene through improvisation was undoubtedly vital. Yet it was only truly beneficial when the decisions that they made on the rehearsal-room floor were grounded in their detailed investigation of the playtext.

The third stage consisted of the actors improvising the scene using their own words, incorporating any of the facts that they could remember. As with the Method of Physical Actions, they might start the improvisations with silent études 'to test [their] understanding of action, counteraction and event' (Carnicke in Hodge 2000: 28).

Following the improvisation, the actors reread the scene and compared it with what they had just experienced. They noted which facts were retained and which were forgotten, and whether the inciting event took place. Rehearsing a play with Active Analysis consisted of repeating this four-stage process of reading, discussing, improvising and discussing. With each new improvisation, the actors strove to add more details of events, language and images.

The fifth and final stage involved memorising the scene. It is important to realise that it wasn't necessary to repeat improvisations ad nauseam. Once the heart of an encounter had been unpacked, the actors could then go away and learn the lines. In fact, if the improvisational work had been successful, they found that the scene had virtually 'learned itself'.

'Here, Today, Now'

The power of Active Analysis lay in its immediacy. It acknowledged the reality of the situation ('Okay, we're on stage, so what shall we do?') and combined it with a sense of playfulness ('But what would we do if . . . ?'). Stanislavsky called it 'Here, Today, Now'. The actors were starting from *themselves*, so they had as much information as they needed to kick-start the creative process into action. Because it was so effortless, the very pleasure of acting and the excitement of live performance became valid emotions in themselves. Whatever the actors had – here, today, now – were the physical and emotional tools with which they worked. This state of being had profound effects both in rehearsal and in performance. *In rehearsal*, the knowledge that the work was simply Active Analysis – in other words, trying out ideas in three dimensions, and not just intellectually – served as a huge liberation for the actors, daring them to be brave in their research. After all: 'A mistake in an *étude* isn't so terrible. The *étude* is a test, a quest, a verification, it is a step towards the creation of a role. It is a rough draft' (Knebel 1981: 17). Actors were therefore free to try ideas out and to reject readily what they had just found out, because all the time their imaginations were working keenly and adaptively.

In performance, the sense of improvisation carried all the way through from first preview to last night. Because the research was always 'Here, Today, Now', the actors took stock of their personal frames of mind each night, noting if they were tired, preoccupied, ill, or just not in the mood. This state then served as the first piece of information, from which the necessary adaptations could easily be made. Just

Figure 1.5 Stanislavsky, aged fifty-five (1918)

like the Method of Physical Actions, Active Analysis was based upon simple actions; therefore, it required no creative 'force' or impossible demands. All the actors had to do was to carry out those simple actions carefully and, as Knebel described it, that action would become their own. Once one simple action (e.g. 'I enter the room') had been accomplished, the second ('I put down my briefcase') followed, then the third ('I kiss my wife), then the fourth and so on. With each action, the actors found that a familiar emotion flared up, and genuine feeling was awakened. It was an easy and effective osmosis from outer action to inner sensation, and back again.

The relevance today

Active Analysis takes pleasure in the simple. Its movement from logical sequence to unexpected experience renders it a remarkably relevant tool for a twenty-first-century performer. Many plays since the 1950s have abandoned a traditional linear plot, with its beginning, middle and end. Therefore, logical sequence isn't necessarily the mainstay of either dramatic structure or the composition of character. Active Analysis accommodates this more anarchic approach and so promises to be the most exciting way in which Stanislavsky's theories can be transported into contemporary theatre practice. Its liberating quality of allowing 'Here, Today, Now' to be sufficient information to begin the creative work is seductively simple to apply in rehearsal, and deliciously enjoyable to experience in performance.

After all the complexities of his theories and systems, it was while exploring the playful elegance of simplicity that Stanislavsky died in 1938. Years of smoking and endless working finally took its toll, and on 2 August he suffered a heart attack at his home, amid the paraphernalia of the Opera-Dramatic Studio. Along with a devoted wife and an extended theatre family, Konstantin Stanislavsky left behind him a teasing quantity of probings into acting and directing, and a number of publications full of tantalising discoveries (see Figure 1.5).

SUMMARY AND ANALYSIS OF *AN ACTOR PREPARES*

INTRODUCTION

Stanislavsky never wanted to thrust his theories into the public domain. Yet the success of the Moscow Art Theatre's American tours in the early 1920s persuaded him otherwise. His autobiography, *My Life in Art*, was the first book to appear in 1924 and, a year later, he began to construct a written version of his highly popular 'system'. His plan was to present the *psychological* preparation of actor-training alongside the *physical* aspect of building a character, with a second book featuring rehearsal practices. This was not to be. The double-pronged fork of inner processes and outer characterisation threatened to prove an impossibly large tome. So the American publishers insisted that Stanislavsky divide the work into two books, with the rehearsal practices comprising a third. Their suggestion was far from satisfactory for Stanislavsky. He was afraid that readers would segregate inner work from external characterisation, whereas he saw them as two sides of the same 'psycho-physical' coin. He reluctantly agreed to the separate volumes (the first to be called *An Actor's Work on Himself in the Creative Process of Experience* and the second *An Actor's Work on Himself in the Creative Process of Physical Characterisation*), only if an outline of all three books was included in the first publication. Unfortunately, Stanislavsky never wrote the overview. And so the very thing that he feared has happened: those of us unable to read the original Russian-language texts have the impression that *An Actor Prepares* (the English translation of the first volume) *is* the 'system'. Therefore, few of us go on to tackle the accompanying *Building a Character* and *Creating a Role*.

An Actor Prepares is certainly rich with goodies concerning Stanislavsky's ideas, as well as being by far the most straightforward of the trilogy. Because it is the book to which most actors and students turn their attention, this chapter will provide a detailed commentary on many of its vivid ideas. At the same time, it is important to remember that *An Actor Prepares* doesn't present the whole picture, and that the three publications feed into each other. Collectively, they provide a thorough picture of Stanislavsky's theories. That said, there are problems with all three books, not least of which is that *Building a Character* and *Creating a Role* are incomplete.

The main concern, though, is the English-language versions. Along with her husband, Norman, the American translator, Elizabeth Reynolds Hapgood, substantially edited the texts, after which further snips were made by the Chief Editor, Edith Isaacs. Although the cuts may seem simple, some of them are particularly unhelpful. One crucial example concerns the Russian text of *An Actor Prepares*, which lists six important questions that all actors must ask of them-selves with each new character. Those questions are: *who*, *when*, *where*, *why*, *for what reason* and *how*. In the English translation, these six questions are given far less attention, with only four of them being summarised (when, where, why and how) (Stanislavsky 1980: 70). Elsewhere in the book, the translation is confusing: in Chapter 10 on 'Communion', the Director (Tortsov) asks the student (Kostya) to 'choose an *object*, with its appropriate, imaginative basis, and to transmit it to him' (Stanislavsky 1980: 219; my emphasis). In fact, a literal translation of the Russian text reads: 'choose an objective'. This is quite a different request, given the psychological motivation implicit in 'objective', but missing in the word 'object'. This example throws up another issue: terminology. Stanislavsky was so keen that his writing-up of the 'system' was not seen as a 'gospel', he chose language that was deliberately accessible to all readers. In the English transla-tion, however, Stanislavsky's simple terms, such as 'bits' of text and 'tasks' for the characters, were subsequently changed to the more scientific-sounding 'units' and 'objectives', creating a different, rather alienating, tone.

These examples of incompatibilities in translation illustrate that some of Stanislavsky's original intentions have become muddied, and for those of us who find the books elusive and sometimes annoying, Stanislavsky is not entirely to blame. Yet if we take a detailed look at the ideas and exercises hidden within, a wealth of wisdom is revealed. . . .

AN ACTOR PREPARES

THE DEVICE

An Actor Prepares takes the form of semi-fictional classes led by the Director, Tortsov, in which his students encounter a series of challenges. Their names reflect their personality traits, and so Tortsov (originally 'Tvortsov') translates as the Creator and the principal student as Kostya Nazvanov, the Chosen One. (Together, they present the voice of Stanislavsky.) Among Kostya's classmates is the ever-questioning Grisha Govorkov (the Chatterbox), the nervous Maria Maloletkova ('of few years') and Nicholas Umnovykh (the Clever-Clogs). Their 'types' throw up different problems in actor-training, and together with Dasha, Leo, Paul, Vanya and the vainglorious Sonya, the classes proceed.

AN OVERVIEW OF THE STRUCTURE

Chapter 1 begins with 'The First Test', for which Tortsov asks each student to select, prepare and present a piece of text. During his 'post-mortem' of the showcase in Chapter 2 ('When Acting is an Art'), Tortsov uses the presentations to identify the students' strengths, weaknesses and personal clichés.

Now their actor-training can proceed in earnest, with the next four chapters focusing on exercises and études to amend the various problems highlighted by the showcase. Tortsov starts with the important component of 'Action' (3), followed by 'Imagination' (4), 'Concentration of Attention' (5) and 'Relaxation of Muscles' (6).

From pure actor-training, the attention turns in Chapter 7 ('Units and Objectives') to textual analysis. In other words, the book takes the idea of each individual having his or her own personality, and connects that individuality with a structured rehearsal technique that has to be adopted by everyone. This connection continues into the next two chapters, with Tortsov stressing in 'Faith and a Sense of Truth' (8) that 'theatrical truth' is not the same as real life. So the students needn't become obsessed with naturalistic detail; instead, their actions on stage should be combined with their own imaginations and 'Emotion Memory' (9).

Having spent the first nine chapters developing the *individual* actor-students, Stanislavsky turns in Chapters 10 to 12 to focus on the *ensemble* and the more 'spiritual' components of acting. 'Communion' (10) invites actors to shift their focus *away* from themselves *towards* their partners, in the belief that the more powerful their on-stage interaction, the more the audience will be magnetised towards their perform-ances. Once the actors are 'communing' with each other, 'Adaptation' (11) challenges them into an even finer quality of listening, so that they can pick up on all the tiny adjustments that they make instinctively in each performance. Finding this degree of attention relies on the sensi-tivity of their 'Inner Motive Forces' (12): *thought*, *feeling* and *will*. This chapter looks at the way in which these inner motive forces first of all interconnect within individual actors, before propelling them into dramatic dialogues with other actors.

The work gradually moves towards performance. 'The Unbroken Line' (13) is remarkably close to the Method of Physical Actions, with references to both the *outer* line of activities that constitute the play's drama, and the *inner* line of psychological actions provided by the actors. Ensuring that these two lines of action remain 'unbroken' requires a strong 'Inner Creative State' (14), which arises in performance when actors mobilise all the components discussed so far (including imagina-tion, attention and relaxation).

The final chapters combine actor-training with rehearsal and per-formance techniques. Chapter 15 suggests that actors must do all the necessary preparation to discover the play's main thrust, or 'The Super-objective'. Then, once it has been identified, the detailed homework can recede from view, and the performers' concentration can focus solely on pursuing that **super-objective**. Ideally, actors then find themselves 'On the Threshold of the Subconscious' (16), where they 'metamorphose' with their characters into the state of 'I am'.

There is a clear journey in *An Actor Prepares* for the students (and the reader) from the ego-driven 'First Test' presentations through inner preparation and textual analysis towards inspirational and unexpected performances. So let's now consider the components in detail.

Chapter 1: 'The First Test'

Kostya's journey through this chapter is painfully recognisable, as he tries his hardest to play Othello and falls into a myriad of traps. His downfall is inevitable, as this is all part of Stanislavsky's storytelling device. After all, Tortsov has set the students up, by insisting that they present their chosen pieces in full costume and make-up and on the theatre's main stage, as the showcase is the only way to 'judge their dramatic quality'. Under such highly competitive conditions, the students' yearning for *results* overrides any kind of *process*.

Kostya's first mistake is to choose a role for which he is far too inexperienced. Within moments of starting to read *Othello*, he dons a bathrobe, grabs a paperknife and prowls round his bedroom like a tiger. Outer image is far more interesting to him than any internal understanding. The following day at the first rehearsal, Kostya tries to repeat his homework, only to find that his private posturings have turned into empty mechanisms. As for paying any attention to Paul as Iago, that seems entirely irrelevant: in fact the text itself seems irrelevant, as Shakespeare's words hardly support Kostya's grand acting. Needless to say, his lack of inner preparation soon takes its toll when, during the dress rehearsal, a nagging voice in his head screams at him: 'Now I'll be stuck!' and instantly he forgets his lines. When it comes to the showcase, Kostya feels completely empty in his performance, and tries to squeeze out the appropriate emotions. Growing increasingly frustrated at his artistic failure, his own anger suddenly turns into Othello's rage towards Desdemona and – with the cry, 'Blood, Iago, blood' – Kostya momentarily fills Shakespeare's dramatic action with his own inner content (see Figure 2.1).

By propelling Kostya into a multitude of clichés, Stanislavsky lures us into a territory with which we feel (embarrassingly) familiar. At the same time, he signposts the major lessons to be learned in the book, such as realising the fragility of a performance based wholly on external effects. Possibly one of the most overt lessons in Chapter 1 concerns discipline: arriving late to class, Kostya is severely reprimanded by the Assistant Director, Rakhmanov, who stresses how difficult it is to arouse a desire to create, and yet how easy it is to kill it. No one has the right to destroy another's creativity by being late. The semi-fictional storytelling device allows Stanislavsky to swipe at the flabby ethics of the nineteenth-century theatre while just steering clear of self-righteousness!

Chapter 2: 'When Acting is an Art'

Having set his students up for a fall in their showcase, Tortsov uses their performances to illustrate five different 'schools' of acting: living a role, representing a role, mechanical acting, overacting and exploitation. It is curious that now – almost a century later – many of his observations are still relevant. The fact that we don't seem much further on in our acting traditions may suggest that Stanislavsky was seeking an ideal school, rather than a possible one; nevertheless, the debate is still hot.

Stanislavsky believed that an actor should aspire to create 'the life of a human spirit' in a beautiful and artistic form. Although this sounds rather esoteric, it boils down to a style of acting in which actors *experience* the role as they create it. That doesn't mean that they have to suffer the painful situations through which their characters might go. It is simpler than that. They just need to be alive to the actual interaction between themselves and their fellow actors. This is Stanislavsky's first 'school' of acting: 'living a role'.

Some actors go through detailed preparation in rehearsal, during which they *do* experience very real emotions analogous to those of their characters. Once they get to performance, however, these actors are only concerned with giving well-crafted *representations* of emotions, not any actual emotion itself. This is Stanislavsky's second 'school' of acting: 'representing a role'. He appreciated the craftsmanship of these actors; yet, he considered the fact that they prevented any real emotion emerging to be just as much of a contortion of natural behaviour as those actors who tried to force their emotions out.

The third 'school', 'mechanical acting', relates very much to the traditional 'types' or *emplois*, where a vocabulary of fixed gestures and 'stencils' has been worked out to replace any real feeling. Nowadays,

Figure 2.1
Stanislavsky as
Othello (1895)

we're no longer convinced by the stock poses of the hand-on-the-heart to represent love, and the back-of-the-hand-to-the-brow to represent grief, and yet the psychological realism of the television age has introduced its own 'stencils', e.g. biting your nails to represent anxious preoccupation, and rubbing your nose to show thoughtfulness.

The fourth 'school', 'overacting', moves down the evolutionary scale as it *'takes the first general human conventions that come along and uses them without even sharpening or preparing them'* (Stanislavsky 1980: 29). As for the fifth 'school', it may be fair to say that, in the age of screen icons and a saturated acting market, 'exploitation' is just as common now as it was in Stanislavsky's time. Exploiters – *'the deadliest enemies of art'* (ibid.: 31) – are those who use acting as a means of exhibiting their beauty, gaining popularity, accruing external success or building a career. Before we go tarring individual actors with a specific 'school' brush, it is worth noting that Stanislavsky believed that each of the five 'schools' coexists within every actor, sometimes even within one performance.

Although it seems rather tagged on at the end of Chapter 2, it is important to recognise that daily lessons in physical disciplines, such as singing, gymnastics, dancing and fencing, are seen as vital counterpoints to Tortsov's psycho-technique.

Chapter 3: 'Action'

In the Russian original, Chapter 3 is called 'Action, If, Given Circumstances', and the importance of all three aspects is certainly reflected in the English translation. However, they aren't the only components of the 'system' to feature heavily here. As Tortsov begins his actor-training programme in earnest, 'imagination', 'feelings', 'inner motives' and 'concentrated attention' are also scattered throughout the chapter. In fact, the division of *An Actor Prepares* into 'Action', 'Relaxation', 'Imagination' and so on can never be clear-cut, as the 'system' is psycho-physical, which means that all the components are interconnected. Nevertheless, Action, If and Given Circumstances dominate this chapter.

The first kind of *action* proposed in Chapter 3 is extremely simple, almost televisual in its intimacy. One by one, Maria, Kostya and Tortsov sit in front of the class and do nothing. While Maria fidgets and looks uncomfortable, Kostya is torn between entertaining the audience and ignoring their presence, but by far the most intriguing subject is Tortsov. He becomes so absorbed in his own inner life that he draws the spectators in: they want to know why he smiled and what was he thinking about, as his physical immobility contained such a powerful intensity.

Stanislavsky then contrasts the 'inner action' sitting exercise with a very physical étude in which Tortsov asks Maria to search for a brooch pinned in the fold of a curtain. Grabbing this opportunity for big dramatic actions, Maria runs to the edge of the footlights and back again, holds her head with her hands and writhes with terror. Afterwards, she is delighted with her on-stage action, and yet . . . she has completely forgotten to find the brooch. The contrast is obvious: Tortsov's sitting exercise illustrated the way in which stillness and simplicity can be completely captivating when there is a psychological and physical *justification* behind even the most imperceptible of actions. Maria's search for the brooch, on the other hand, demonstrated how unimpressive excessive movement and 'suffering' can be when actors fail to connect with what they are doing. In a precursor to the Method of Physical Actions, Tortsov emphasises the value of action over feeling, insisting that his students shouldn't strive 'to be jealous, or make love, or to suffer, for its own sake' (Stanislavsky 1980: 41): i.e. don't 'play emotion'. If they pursue their actions imaginatively and truthfully, they can't help but arouse the appropriate emotions.

Following the two examples of 'Action', Stanislavsky then takes us on to 'If'. Tortsov simply asks 'What would you do *if* there was a madman behind the door?' and the students improvise their responses to the Madman étude. 'If' is an extremely powerful tool: without forcing actors to do anything, it easily and instantly incites them to action, by posing the question, 'What would you *do* if . . . ?' Throughout *An Actor Prepares*, Stanislavsky emphasises the importance of emotion in actors and here he offers 'If' as the most direct and natural means of arousing true feelings. If the students really imagine what they would do *if* there was a madman behind the door, they will soon feel excitement and fear, and want to do something about it.

Closely joined to 'If' are what the celebrated Russian poet, Aleksandr Pushkin (1799–1837), called the 'Given Circumstances'. The 'Given Circumstances' are all the details that arise from the play, as well as the suggestions provided by the director (including set, costumes and lighting) and the actors' own ideas about the script and the characters. While 'If' is the starting point for the imagination, the 'Given Circumstances' water that imaginative seed.

By means of these three components ('Action', 'If' and the 'Given Circumstances'), Stanislavsky invites actors to percolate the fictions of the play ('Given Circumstances') through their own imaginations ('If') to stimulate believable 'Actions' and 'feelings that seem true' (Stanislavsky 1980: 51). What Stanislavsky is doing through his 'system' is examining spontaneous natural behaviour, taking it apart, then putting it back together. In this way, actors can begin to control processes, which would otherwise be intuitive and haphazard: he calls it 'unconscious creativeness through conscious technique' (ibid.: 50).

Chapter 4: 'Imagination'

Again, in Chapter 4, it is clear to see how the components of the 'system' can't be entirely separated. Although 'Imagination' is the focal point here, 'action', 'sense memory', 'adaptation' and 'the unbroken line' are also brought in. The premise in this chapter is that real life is converted into theatrical reality by means of imagination, which, like any physical muscle, has to be exercised and developed.

Tortsov's first lesson in imagination begins very simply by turning the students' attention to the present situation: an afternoon acting class. He then *adapts* one given circumstance – the time of day – and quizzes them as to how they would change their behaviour if in fact it were three o'clock in the morning. The next task is a little more complex: using his imagination, Kostya is asked to take the group into his bedroom, moment by moment, detail by detail. This process requires him to describe a logical, coherent series of small imagined actions (such as opening the door and turning on the light), in order to stimulate more sophisticated, emotional responses (such as excitement, anxiety or comfort). At one point, Kostya finds his imagination completely dries up when he suggests that he hang himself in his closet. Herein lies the importance of logic; after all: 'It is only reasonable that your imagination should balk at being asked to work from *a doubtful premise* to *a stupid conclusion*' (Stanislavsky 1980: 62; my emphasis). We can see that this is the basis of the Method of Physical Actions, as Tortsov highlights the actors' need for a psychological coherence as much as a logical sequence of external actions. Later in Stanislavsky's book, a whole chapter is devoted to 'the unbroken line' of inner/outer actions, yet it is worth noting that its roots lie here with the development of imagination.

Possibly the most useful aspect of his Chapter 4 is the attention drawn to six fundamental questions: *Who* am I? *Where* am I? *When* am I here? *Why* am I here (i.e. What *past* circumstances have led to me being here)? *For what reason* am I here (i.e. What do I want to achieve *now* I am here and what *future* actions should I carry out to achieve that result)? And *How* shall I go about it (i.e. What are those future actions)? An exercise is set up in which Paul has to imagine himself as an oak tree, finding appropriate answers to the Six Questions. Stanislavsky deliberately chooses something as passive as 'being an oak tree' in order to illustrate that, even in the most improbable of situations, a vibrant imagination will always arouse a desire for action. Of these Six Questions, Tortsov stresses that '*for what reason*' is extremely important: it is the question that catapults actors towards 'an active goal' – or 'objective'. To find the most burning answer to this question, actors have to add something personal from their own lives, something which will trigger their genuine desire to fulfil the objective. Paul, for example, is excited by fights; so Tortsov suggests that he imagines the oak tree being under attack. Having found something that really excites him, Paul can then invest it in his imaginary circumstances (in this case, 'being an oak tree') to fuel his desire for action.

The 'message' of this chapter seems to be that the more the answers to the Six Questions are rooted in personal material, the more powerful will be the actors' imaginative connection with the given circumstances.

Chapter 5: 'Concentration of Attention'

This is probably one of the most straightforward chapters in the book, exploring how to develop concentration, observation and imagination in order to strengthen 'attention' on stage. Here the idea of the 'fourth wall' (the invisible wall between the audience and the stage) is introduced. This aspect of the 'system' has been much maligned, but it is important to remember that, for Stanislavsky, the audience played a vital part in live performance, and references to their significance are scattered throughout *An Actor Prepares* (particularly in Chapter 10, 'Communion'). At the same time, Stanislavsky was waging a war against exploitative actors and the 'star system', where performers connected with an audience for their own personal acclaim, rather than for serving the playwright's text. Stanislavsky wanted to focus the actors' attention back on to the stage. But how should he go about it?

In this chapter, Stanislavsky (via Tortsov) starts by setting up the 'Money-burning étude', in which Kostya's 'moron' brother throws wads of money on to a fire and watches with delight as they burn. The students play out the improvisation three times on the stage: once with the curtain up, once with the curtain down and once under the illusion that they're entirely on their own. (Secretly, they are being spied on by Tortsov and Rakhmanov.) During each variation, they fail to excite themselves with any sense of truth in their actions. And yet, when they are told to find out which one of them has lost a shoe-heel, their attention is instantly engaged, leaving them oblivious to the extraneous activity going on in the auditorium. Here then lies the antidote to un-focused attention: a genuine activity, with a real purpose, that wholly absorbs the actors' concentration.

The chapter continues to explore how stage attention operates and dissipates, beginning with *Points of Light* which dart around the whole theatre to highlight the way in which most actors' focus flits from stage to auditorium and back again. Having used the Points of Light to illus-trate the waywardness of their attention, Tortsov develops the students' concentration by means of shifting *Circles of Attention*. They begin with the Small Circle, in which they simply focus on a space that encom-passes their own heads and hands; this creates a sense of Solitude in Public – of being alone although they are being watched. This space then expands to the Medium Circle (the individual actor and the nearby environment), then the Large Circle (the stage space) and finally the very Largest Circle (stage and auditorium).

Towards the latter part of the chapter, Stanislavsky draws an important difference between *external* attention (which focuses on objects, furniture and people) and *inner* attention (which works together with sense memory and imagination). Tortsov offers some exercises for refining inner attention, including remembering every-thing that has happened that day by recalling rooms and picturing people. Although this sounds very simple, Tortsov points out that inner exercises are much harder than physical drills; the mind is very tricksy and likes to wander all over the place, rather than getting on with the mental task. That said, inner attention is like imagination – it is a muscle that can be strengthened by daily 'workouts', as long as the actor is determined and patient.

Chapter 6: 'Relaxation of Muscles'

Although *An Actor Prepares* is primarily concerned with psychological preparation and *Building a Character* with physical preparation, Chapter 6 draws the two together. In the middle of the previous chapter, Kostya drops in the fact that halfway through their acting lesson, the students went away for a dance class before returning to their concentration exercises. Although the remark is thrown in casually, it is of course deliberate, as it reminds us that the acting classes led by Tortsov and the drills led by his assistant, Rakhmanov, are not the be-all and end-all of the 'system'. Physical training is equally important. To take this point further, Stanislavsky uses the device of Kostya being too tense on stage and accidently grazing an artery to highlight the need for muscular relaxation.

The message of Chapter 6 is simple: you can't do 'inner work' if you're physically too tense. The point is confirmed when the students take turns at lifting a piano, at the same time as trying to remember tastes, smells and textures or doing mental arithmetic. They can't do it! There follows a series of simple relaxation exercises (detailed in Chapter 4 of this book, p. 118), which are designed to develop within each actor a 'controller'. The 'controller' is an inner voice which rings alarm bells at any moment when unnecessary tension creeps into your body.

'Relaxation of Muscles' also involves imagination, and for the first time 'objectives' are introduced into the terminology. An exercise is set up in which a number of poses are struck, so that the actors can observe which muscles are *necessarily* contracted and which are *unduly* tense. Tortsov then repeats the exercise with the added ingredient that each new pose has to be informed by an 'imaginative idea' and a 'given circumstance'. So an arm is not just lifted, it is raised to grab a peach from a tree. This combination of imaginative idea and given circumstance is referred to by Tortsov as an 'actual objective'. As soon as the students invest their physical actions with an actual objective, they discover that all their superfluous tension ebbs away and they only use the muscles that are necessary. We see clearly here how the 'system' is inherently psycho-physical. As soon as Stanislavsky addresses physical training, he instantly interweaves imaginative motives; so each physical exercise has a psychological backdrop to ease the body's difficulties or tensions.

Towards the end of the chapter, an invaluable exercise is introduced, one which could easily be overlooked on a cursory reading. It involves what Rakhmanov calls an 'isolated act'. The students are simply asked to raise their right arms, using only the isolated muscle group needed for the action, while he checks their backs and necks for undue tension. Once they have explored the whole arm, they break the movement down to try other joints: the elbow, the wrist and the various bones in the hands. The movements are then combined to form a 'wave motion' up the arm, from shoulder to finger tips and back again. (This exercise is included in Chapter 4 of this book, p. 137.) To the students' astonishment, they are hopeless at the sequence.

Breaking movements down into 'isolated acts' is a vital aspect of fine-tuning the body to be an effective psycho-physical instrument. Actors need clarity and flexibility of both inner and outer actions if the way in which they incarnate their characters is to be precise and artistic. This is psycho-physical training at its most vital: the actors' inner sensations and the outer expression of those sensations are inextricably linked through simple technical exercises (like the 'isolated act'). This develops their inner–outer coordination. After all, Stanislavsky saw physical stiffness as a reflection of emotional inflexibility. However, it requires extremely attentive reading of *An Actor Prepares* to pick up on all the nuances of these exercises, and to assess how they fit into the development of Stanislavsky's 'system'. It is much easier to understand the bolder examples, such as Kostya's observation of his cat: we can all identify with his astonishment at how his cat can move from complete repose to lightning movement with an absolute economy of energy and no extraneous muscular tension.

It's a nice touch when, at the end of the chapter, Kostya reveals his developing self-awareness through his comment on their first showcase: 'What a good lesson the Director gave us in that test performance, when we all did the wrong things with complete assurance. It was a wise and convincing way of proving his point' (Stanislavsky 1980: 110).

Chapter 7: 'Units and Objectives'

At the beginning of Chapter 7, Tortsov congratulates his students on arriving at a new and important stage in their work, that stage being textual analysis. For a twenty-first-century reader, this is possibly the most accessible and instantly usable part of the 'system', though perhaps the trickiest problem is the terminology itself. Frequently throughout this chapter, 'units' are also referred to as 'bits' (which is in fact a literal translation of the Russian *kusok*), and the original word *zadacha* doesn't actually translate as 'objective', but as 'goal' or 'task'. For the purposes of this analysis, however, we'll stick to 'objectives' and 'units', although Stanislavsky's less scientific 'bits' and 'tasks' are far more useful in practice.

First of all, Stanislavsky uses the idea of carving up a turkey to clarify what he means by 'units'. Just as you can't eat a turkey all in one go (you have to cut it into wings, legs and breast, and then into smaller, chewable pieces), neither can you 'devour' an entire play at one sitting. As actors, you have to divide it into bite-size chunks or 'units'. Then – just as mouthfuls of turkey are flavoured by gravy, sauce and mustard – the 'units' are coloured by imagination, 'If', the given circumstances, notes from the director and the contribution of the actors themselves.

To identify the large units of a play, the actors ask the question: *'What is the core of the play – the thing without which it cannot exist?'* (Stanislavsky 1980: 115–16). Once the large divisions have been identified, medium and small units within those larger sections are then determined. Stanislavsky is keen to point out that dividing the play into units is only a temporary measure simply to ease rehearsal work and, although it is vital that the labels are precise, actors mustn't be strait-jacketed by too much detail. To prevent this, they need to hang on to the idea of a *channel* which streamlines and focuses all the tiny actions within the larger units. The 'channel' idea is made clearer by the image of Kostya walking home. Initially, from opening the front door as he leaves his friends' flat to getting into bed back at home, Kostya accumulates 216 units. This is far too many to be useful, so Tortsov boils this number down to four by carving out the *channel*: (1) Kostya leaves the flat to walk home; (2) he looks in a bookshop window; (3) he gets ready for bed; and (4) he lies in bed thinking. Underpinning this channel of units is his main *creative objective*: 'to get home to bed'.

Defining a character's 'creative objective' is arguably one of the most significant contributions that Stanislavsky made to modern acting practice, and he suggests that on stage, as in life, we pursue three different kinds of objectives: 'mechanical', 'rudimentary psychological' and 'psychological'. 'Mechanical objectives' are essentially ritualistic in their content: for example, I meet someone for the first time and I shake her hand. My action has no particular psychological content: my objective is simply 'I wish to make her acquaintance' and, at this stage, I invest the ritual handshake with no particular personal emotion. I am then introduced to a famous actor, for whom I have an immense regard: my objective, as I shake his hand, is that 'I wish to express my respect'. Now there is a 'rudimentary psychological' investment in my hand-shake, raising it from the simple mechanical ritual of the first encounter. Finally, I meet a friend with whom I had a terrible row yesterday: as I shake her hand, my objective is that 'I wish to reassure her that our friendship is still intact and I apologise for the incident'. Involved in the simple sequence of actions (including lifting my hand, making contact with hers and endowing the handshake with my sense of reassurance and apology) is a very complex personal process. This objective is clearly an inner, 'psychological' one. Stanislavsky draws our attention to these three different encounters to illustrate just how simple objectives can be, and also how wonderfully liquid are the lines between physicality and psychology. So we don't have to struggle too hard to be 'psycho-physical' actors!

Since objectives are so critical for performance, Stanislavsky spends some time in Chapter 7 defining them and articulating how they should be named. The quickest way to discover a character's objective is to ask the question: 'What do I want?' But the answer can't be too general – for example, 'I want power' – since that in itself isn't dynamic enough. The vital question would need to be something like: 'What must I do to obtain that power?' Only active questions will produce exciting and magnetic objectives, and expressing the objective through a verb ensures that it is forward-moving and attractive to the actor doing it. In fact, Tortsov lists nine qualities that a creative objective must possess, the first of which is that it should be directed towards the on-stage partner, not out into the auditorium. Second, it must be linked to the actor's own emotional/experiential repertoire to make it meaningful for the actor, and, third, it needs to be creative and artistic. The fourth point is that it should be real and human, not theatrical and dead, and (point five) it must be something that the actor can believe in. (Only then will the on-stage partners and the audience be able to believe in it too.) Sixth, it needs to be attractive to the actor, otherwise there is no point in choosing it, and seventh, it should be precise and relevant to the character, rather than for the actor's own exhibitionism. The penultimate point is that it must have a value and an inner content, and not be shallow or artificial, and finally – and most importantly – it must be *active* and *forward-moving*; after all, objectives form the back-bone of the play's dramatic action. Finding an objective that contains all these qualities may strike us as terrifyingly daunting. However, it's not that difficult if you remember that even the most simple physical objective (like the handshake) contains within it a psychological component. So you may think that your chosen objective is simplistic and physical, but if you do it sincerely and direct it towards your on-stage partner, you will soon sense its profound psychological reverberations.

Many twenty-first-century practitioners spend time in rehearsals naming objectives; yet all too easily they fall into the trap of turning it into a rather dry, intellectual process. In Chapter 7, Stanislavsky insists that naming objectives should be active and emotive, in order to excite the actors who have to perform the play. Usually the label that you choose for a particular *unit* will reveal to you the characters' *objectives*. That said, there are two important points to be raised here. First of all, while you may express the unit as a noun (an intellectual concept), the objective must be expressed as a verb (forward-moving action). Second, you will quickly find that each character within a particular unit has a different objective; so while the name of the *unit* will be the same for the two characters, the labels for their *objectives* could be totally contradictory. After all, dramatic tension arises from one character trying to achieve an objective while being constantly blocked by another character pursuing a different one. The main message of this chapter seems to be that, if your objectives don't excite you as an actor, then scrap them and start again: textual analysis is a passionate affair, not an academic exercise!

Chapter 8: 'Faith and a Sense of Truth'

Twice as long as any other section of *An Actor Prepares*, Chapter 8 is full of rather esoteric ideas, which Stanislavsky attempts to clarify with varying degrees of success. So we'll try and elucidate them here! Two

Figure 2.2 Stanislavsky as Ananyi in Pisemsky's *Bitter Fate* (1888)

key études dominate the chapter: the Money-burning Scene (which emphasises the interplay of action and imagination in a prototype of the Method of Physical Actions), and a scene from Ibsen's *Brand* (which implicitly draws emotion memory into the equation). Both of these études will be looked at in detail, but at the heart of the chapter lies the inherent contradiction of acting: that 'everything must be *real* in the *imaginary* life of the actor' (Stanislavsky 1980: 157; my emphasis). In unpacking this contradiction, Tortsov differentiates between the 'actual fact' of real life, where we never know what will happen next, and the 'scenic truth' of theatrical fiction, where the actors create the *illusion* of not knowing what will happen next. To clarify the territory, Tortsov then unravels the two terms featured in the chapter's title: a 'sense of truth' and 'faith'. And very quickly the psycho-physical dimensions become apparent. . . .

A sense of truth depends on physical, naturalistic details, which actors draw from real life to provide both themselves and the audience with a feeling of authenticity – that 'this looks like something that we recognise from real life'. *Faith* or *belief* is the psychological component added by the actors to these external details. The two elements, *external truth* and *internal belief*, combine to convince the audience that the fictional events that they see on stage could actually happen.

Attached to truth and faith is a third element: a *sense of untruth*. For the audience, the 'sense of untruth' is that they know they are in a theatre; therefore, these events are not *really* happening and yet they suspend their disbelief and commit to the theatrical deceit. For the actors, the 'sense of untruth' is a useful tool to prevent them from 'acting too much'. Tortsov points out that often actors are so keen to convince themselves and the audience that what they are doing is entirely sincere, that they begin to *over*act, and inadvertently fall into mechanical acting to make up for the fact that what they are doing isn't *really* real. Tortsov's advice is to remain 'cool and impartial'. Several times in this chapter, he instructs his students to 'Cut ninety per cent!', believing that simplicity on stage is far more compelling than over-naturalistic detail. The example that Tortsov uses is the woman who, when told of her husband's death, remains almost statuesquely still: she is in a state of 'tragic inaction'. (The character portrayed by Stanislavsky in Figure 2.2 enscapsulates a similar sense of 'tragic inaction'.)

In exploring 'truth' and 'faith', Stanislavsky homes in on an early kind of Method of Physical Actions, seen here in terms of what he calls 'the life of the human body' and 'the creation of the human soul'. Returning to the Money-burning étude, Tortsov asks Kostya to act out the counting of the money without any actual props, just using his imagination. He must mime every detail of unwrapping the bundles, discarding the string and smoothing out the creased bank notes with absolute accuracy; only then will he strengthen his sense of truth. In other words, he has to create a believable sequence of physical actions, which he can repeat over and over until the sequence is familiar. Each time, he must note the new sensations that arise and how those sensations propel him forward with increasing conviction. This is undoubtedly the process behind the Method of Physical Actions: the main emphasis here is on the physical, external details of the scene to create the *life of the human body*.

Yet there is still *the creation of the human soul* to consider. But that is not as difficult as it sounds. If the actors commit to the sequence of physical actions with utter conviction, then they should find that genuine emotions arise, and these emotions soak into their external actions. This in itself is the *creation of the human soul*. In a nutshell, Tortsov invites his students to begin with a simple line of achievable physical actions, through which he leads them towards big emotional experiences without arousing any muscular tension or psychological alarm. Yet another aspect of the 'system' is seen to be psycho-physical, with body and psychology interdepending.

From action to imagination to emotion. . . . We now come to a kind of prototype of Active Analysis in what is one of the most important but complicated sections of the chapter. It involves an étude using the scene from Ibsen's *Brand* when Agnes finds the baby; in this étude, Dasha improvises with a stick for a baby. The section needs careful reading to understand the point being made, as an imprecise reading could convince us that Stanislavsky is encouraging the painful dredging-up of emotion memories on stage. So let's take a closer look. . . .

Dasha enacts the scene five times. The first time, she instinctively connects her own emotions with the circumstances of the scene, weeping profusely and successfully drawing in the audience. She then insists on immediately re-enacting the scene to demonstrate how powerful her inspiration is, and yet she finds she can't infuse it with anything and so she stops herself. (The important thing to note is that, despite the emptiness of her second improvisation, her first attempt had shown Tortsov the capacity of her emotion-centre.) In her third go,

Dasha works through the physical actions of the scene with a certain amount of truth and belief, but she fails to respond to the stick as if it were a child; consequently, the scene never really takes off. In her fourth étude, she *consciously* tries to recall what she went through *instinctively* during her first improvisation, and she quickly finds herself weeping, though this time the audience is untouched. This maybe because she is 'playing her own emotion', rather than taking the spectators on the necessary emotional journey. Finally, Tortsov gives an imaginative suggestion (that Dasha herself has lost a child), which happens to coincide with a real incident from Dasha's life (when she miscarried a baby). Because the imaginative suggestion overlaps so much with a real emotion memory, Dasha begins to weep and the scene again becomes very powerful to watch.

Kostya argues that it wasn't the physical actions that prompted Dasha's emotional experience, but the painful imaginative stimulus provided by Tortsov. Tortsov agrees, but emphasises that he deliberately introduced the imaginative stimulus at a very specific point in rehearsals: Dasha had already shown him (in Impro 1) that her emotional resources were active, and she had also discovered (in Impro 3) a convincing and detailed line of physical actions. She just needed a 'trigger' to get her back in touch with the scene in a way that would embrace the audience (which clearly her tears in Impro 4 failed to do). Through the help of Tortsov's imaginative provocation, Dasha was able to reconnect with her emotions by harnessing them together with her already rehearsed actions and her open creative imagination. Had it been nothing but her personal emotion memory, Dasha's tears would have been completely inappropriate, as they would have been her own tears for the loss of her own child rather than Agnes's joy at discovering the baby on the doorstep. Again, she would have been 'playing her own emotion', instead of creating the right emotional path for the audience to travel along. Tortsov suggests that Impro 5 was quite 'safe', as at no point was Dasha 'hallucinating' or overwhelmed by her emotions. She never actually believed that the stick was really her child, but, rather, she believed in the possibility of what would happen if the fictional events in the play should occur in her own life.

The ideas explored in the Dasha–baby étude are perplexingly muddied, as evidently Stanislavsky himself was grappling with complicated nuances for which there was no rock-solid vocabulary. Suffice it to say, this section of the book should be treated with caution! Far more accessible is Grisha Govorkov's frustration with the endless attention to detail demanded by Tortsov in creating a sense of truth and belief. When his acting is constantly criticised, Grisha declares: 'Art is free! It needs space, and not your little physical truths. We must be free for great [flights], instead of crawling around like little beetles' (Stanislavsky 1980: 158). (NB: The English version mistranslates 'flights' as 'fights'.) Here Stanislavsky uses the character of Grisha to make the point that great acting isn't entirely spontaneous. The flight path from tangible physical action to spiritual, exalted art needs precision and detail. Grisha is an example of the 'representational actor' discussed in Chapter 2 of *An Actor Prepares*. He represents images and passions in his acting, whereas Tortsov looks for the actual recreation of those images and passions. Grisha deals in appearances; Tortsov seeks realities. For Grisha, the audience are onlookers; for Tortsov, the audience are an active part of the creative processes, because they *believe* in the possibility of what they see on stage.

Although Chapter 8 is difficult to unpack, the basic components are very useful. Yet again, various aspects of the 'system' are seen to interconnect intricately. Faith and a sense of truth are created when even the smallest physical movements are injected into the given circumstances of the play, and they can 'acquire great significance through their influence on emotion' (Stanislavsky 1980: 149). From the line of actions to moments of inspiration, from naturalistic detail to psychological reverberations, from the actor's physical body to the character's human soul: Stanislavsky calls this process of action and the actors' belief in that action, 'our method of psycho-technique' (ibid.: 151).

Chapter 9: 'Emotion Memory'

'Emotion memory' is a tricky aspect of Stanislavsky's 'system', often misunderstood by practitioners, who either place too much significance on its use or who dismiss it out of hand as psychologically unhealthy. Stanislavsky actually contradicts himself at times in Chapter 9, which increases the confusion; added to which, the English translation is often misleading. So let's try and clarify some of the difficulties.

Returning to the Madman étude (see p. 47), the students find that, although they thoroughly enjoy their improvisation, they are repeating actions and reactions from a previous version; the result is that they give an accurate, ready-made *form* of the exercise but it lacks any inner *content.* Tortsov uses their findings as an illustration of how acting becomes mechanical and formal when actors don't invest their performances with their own human responses. At this point in the book, the concept of 'emotion memory' (or 'affective memory') is explicitly introduced. The term is adopted from the French psychologist, Théodule Ribot (see Chapter 1, p. 16), who discovered that, if patients remembered times when they were healthy, they recovered faster than those patients who engaged less actively in their own process of recovery. The effect of past-tense memories on present-tense circumstances was applied by Stanislavsky to fictional situations in drama.

He separated out two kinds of affective memory – 'sense memory' and 'emotion memory'. Sense (or sensation) memory involves a process of consciously recalling the sights and sounds from the original experience to excite sensations here and now. (Taste, touch and smell are also components in sense memory, although Stanislavsky suggests that they are less powerful and more auxiliary.) Emotion memory has a more psychological, less tangible quality than sense memory: often when we recall past experiences, we find that the feelings conjured up are now stronger, weaker or simply different from the original, but that change is perfectly valid. In fact, it is not just the feelings that change. The memories themselves don't remain fixed: they merge with each other and with our imaginations. That is not to say the memories become weakened, but, rather, our responses as actors to emotional nuances have to become more sensitive.

The transitions don't stop there. Stanislavsky didn't want emotion memories to remain too personal or parochial: ideally, they should take on a wider significance. He illustrates what he means by this through Kostya's experience of a street accident. When Kostya sees an old man knocked over by a streetcar, he becomes aware of the colours of the incident; those colours provoke memories and at the same time become symbols of universal 'themes'. The white snow reminds him of life, the dark figure of death, the stream of blood of the old man's transgressions, the sun and sky of the eternity of the world, and the passing cars of passing generations. In other words, the naturalistic, sensory details of the incident pass into Kostya's imagination, moving from a literal to a psychological and imaginative plane, which then expands into wider – symbolic – reverberations. Added to this, Kostya finds that, when he recalls the incident, his memory merges with other impressions, such as the time he saw an old Italian feeding orange rind to a dead monkey. So the power of an emotion memory needn't necessarily lie in the remembered details of the original experience, but, rather, in the connections that the actor's imagination makes and the resonances of those connections.

Emotional recall is, therefore, not an end in itself – it is the fine-tuning of an actor's psycho-physical sensitivity; it is the mixing of colours in the actor's imaginative palette. As Stanislavsky puts it, emotion memory 'is a kind of synthesis of memory on a large scale. It is purer, more condensed, compact, substantial and sharper than the actual happenings' (Stanislavsky 1980: 173). The subtle transformations of emotion memories can be exciting and fruitful, and through their permutations they can build up an actor's personal repertoire. It's worth remembering this when you're trying to recall the death of your dog in order to transfer that emotion to the on-stage drama. Maybe you can find a more colourful stimulus. . . .

In fact, stimuli needn't be internal. Often the very technical aspects of the production itself can provoke your emotions. This is demonstrated in *An Actor Prepares* by a very simple improvisation. The students are asked to sit in Maria's fictitious apartment (used in a number of études), while the lighting and soundscape change from early morning to midnight within a matter of minutes. They make a note of their personal reactions, discovering that the early morning conjures up a host of sensations and memories that differ considerably from the atmosphere of late evening. Through this exercise, the actors experience the way in which emotion and sense memory can be provoked without any force or psychological contortion, but by simply attending to the external changes in atmosphere incurred through lighting and sound.

The power of external staging on emotion memory is demonstrated even more intriguingly through a series of improvisations, which – if we examine it carefully – reveals another early form of Active Analysis. In Step 1, Tortsov begins by inviting each of the students to sit anywhere they like as long as they are near him. In other words, they spontaneously create a *mise-en-scène* according to how they each feel towards him, using the present tense (here and now) as the basis for the stage picture. Tortsov then creates a number of simple settings with a few pieces of furniture: this is Step 2. He asks the students to say what mood, emotions or sensations are aroused within each of them by the arrangement, and to imagine under what circumstances they would use the furniture in the way that it is set out. The psychological journey is therefore from outer stimulus (the furniture) to spontaneous inner sensation, then to imagination and potential action. Tortsov creates some new arrangements in Step 3 and this time he tells the students how they are to use the furniture, and they have to say what emotional circumstances they would have to create in order to use the set to fit his instructions. In other words, he tells them where to go on the set and they have to justify to themselves (by finding an appropriate 'objective') why they are making the required moves. Stanislavsky suggests that this is what normally goes on in rehearsals: the director tells the actors where to go (or what the 'blocking' is) and they have to obey his instructions. To make sure that their movements aren't mechanical, they have to find reasons and objectives in which they can fully believe, so that their reactions are alive with emotions. Step 4 involves Tortsov putting the students on the set in positions which deliberately oppose their objectives and moods. They experience the contradiction between how they feel (their inner state) and the positions in which they are put (their outer reality) and then somehow they have to motivate the actions provided by the director to express their objectives. This four-stage sequence of exercises warms the actors up psycho-physically. It alerts them to the way in which they as actors have to find appropriate *mises-en-scène* that fit their objectives and moods; at the same time, they have to be able to find objectives and moods that fill in a *mise-en-scène* when it has been imposed from the outside by a dictatorial director. This sequence of exercises unlocks the processes of Active Analysis, where external action and internal sensation have to work in harmony, even when there are inherent contradictions.

Possibly one of the most important lessons to emerge from the chapter on 'Emotion Memory' is that the process is more important than the result. The result (the emotion) will only arise if the process (the actions) are appropriate and executed with a sense of truth and faith. Since actors will only be as rich as their personal 'palettes', Tortsov encourages his students to build up their emotional repertoires through books, arts, science, travel, museums and – of course – through other people. Once the actors' sensory sensitivity has been awakened, they will discover that, on stage, there are six primary emotional stimuli: (1) the suggestions from their imagination and from external realities; (2) 'units and objectives'; (3) objects of attention on stage and in the audience; (4) physical actions founded in truth and executed with belief; (5) the playtext itself and the characters' thoughts, feelings and interrelationships; and (6) the set with the addition of lighting and sound. These six stimuli Tortsov calls the 'psycho-technical store of riches' (Stanislavsky 1980: 191): if actors are open to the range of stimuli around them, then almost anything can prompt an emotional response.

There are myths surrounding emotion memory, in which actors believe that 'playing emotion' lies at the heart of convincing acting. Wrong! A careful reading of Chapter 9 dispels those myths, highlighting the way in which emotion memory interconnects with action, imagina-tion and textual analysis. The chapter reveals Stanislavsky's awareness that emotion memories constantly change. It is the actor's suscepti-bility to those changes (as much as the details of the memory itself) that lies at the heart of emotional recall. We are also given an insight into Stanislavsky's obsession with naturalistic detail: he saw those everyday details as being a vital part of the process of luring and exciting emotions in actors, and not just as a startling stage effect. Therefore, even in a chapter devoted to emotion memory, we see that the outer world (set, props, lighting, sound and actions) and the inner world (imagination, emotions and objectives) are inextricably linked in a psycho-physical dialogue.

Chapter 10: 'Communion'

Many of the components of Stanislavsky's 'system' seem quite esoteric and hard to pin down from a simple reading of An Actor Prepares, perhaps none more so than 'communion', and yet it is actually quite straight-forward. Like emotion memory, communion (or 'irradiation') focuses on filling external actions with inner content, the difference being that the actors' attention is now turned outwards towards the other actors and not inwards towards their own memories. At this point in An Actor Prepares, Stanislavsky introduces the 'unbroken line of attention' (the focus of Chapter 13) to elucidate the fact that an actor's concentration is like a string of gold beads. If you break the line of concentration, then it is as if every third bead is made of tin. You really have to 'touch' your partner with your text; after all, if drama is about communication between characters, acting must be about genuine communion between actors. Only when actors can convince each other of their objectives through an uninterrupted exchange of thoughts and actions will the spectators be convinced by what they see on stage. So communion, therefore, operates on two simultaneous levels: directly between the actors and indirectly with the audience, whom Stanislavsky describes as the 'spiritual acoustics' (Stanislavsky 1980: 204).

Given the Soviet censorship of the time, Stanislavsky is very adventurous in his choice of vocabulary here. He refers to the Hindu *prana* energy centre in the solar plexus as the point from which actors have to connect if they are going to be in genuine communion with each other. The prana energy centre is the touchstone for feeling the difference between communication and communion, and Stanislavsky proffers two particular exercises for the students to experience that difference. The first exercise involves them 'arguing' in pairs. At first Kostya relies on his wrists and fingers to communicate his point, and so Tortsov restricts his use of gestures. To compensate for having no gestures, he raises his voice too much. Then Tortsov ties him to a chair and he can only use his face. Finally, his face is covered up, so that the only tool he has for arguing is a roar! When Tortsov asks him which means of communication he would like to have restored, he replies 'all of them', as he has begun to understand the genuine power of each tool, whether it be gestures, face or voice. The second exercise relies on communion. Kostya is asked to think of an objective and to convey it to Tortsov first of all via words, gestures and facial expressions. Then, one by one, his means of communication are restricted until, finally, he can only express his objective through silently sending out rays of energy to his partner and trying hard to absorb the rays of energy that his partner is sending back. Although it sounds difficult, it's not impossible (see Chapter 4, this volume, pp. 149–50). For Tortsov, this exchange of energy is the 'unbroken line of communion': he insists that, even when text and movement are added, the unbroken reception and emission of rays of energy (underlying the spoken dialogue) should always be maintained.

Possibly one of Stanislavsky's most useful terms for describing 'communion' is **grasp**: 'grasp' is 'what a bull-dog has in his jaw. We actors must have the same power to seize with our eyes, ears and all our senses' (Stanislavsky 1980: 217). Being in someone's 'grasp' is not an uncommon experience, whether it be a great storyteller, a close-up magician, a true love, or a mesmeric actor! As a performer, you can sense when you have the audience in your grasp, 'eating out of your hand'. Grasp is, in fact, incredibly effortless, requiring no extraneous physical exertion. You just need a great sense of inner activity, achieved by having an interesting objective, which totally absorbs you, both in your actions and in your partners. Curiously, 'grasp' is rarely mentioned in books about Stanislavsky; yet when, in Chapter 15, he lists the three most important features of creative acting, the first to be mentioned is 'inner grasp' (ibid.: 279). The term 'grasp' is far more accessible than either 'communion' or 'irradiation', and gives us a concept with which we can instantly connect: 'Am I in your grasp? Are you in my grasp? Are we *really* listening and connecting with each other?'

Stanislavsky stresses how important it is to practise these communion exercises with real, living people – not alone, or with imaginary characters – as it is easy for actors to delude themselves that they have found a sense of 'grasp' when actually it is nothing more than muscular tension. Ideally, early exercises in communion should be supervised by someone who can notice the differences between grasp and tension. That is why this chapter is extremely important but very difficult: the issues can't be communicated satisfactorily through the written page, and it takes an adventurous director to give them a go and let the actors find out just how powerful genuine communion can be. But it's worth it! The chapter concludes with a useful summary of the two different kinds of exercises. The first are those in which the actors concentrate on objectives and convey them to each other through emitting and absorbing rays, while also paying attention to the physical sensations that arise. The second are those in which the actors make no attempt to convey a particular objective: it's simply a question of giving out and receiving rays in order to experience the different sensations between real communion and muscular tension.

Chapter 11: 'Adaptation'

'Communion' and 'Adaptation' are absolutely interdependent: 'as long as we are on the stage we are in unending contact with one another, therefore our adjustments to each other must be constant' (Stanislavsky 1980: 234). In describing adaptation, Tortsov refers to five vital components: we have to (1) adjust to the given circumstance or problem of the scene; (2) express what is going on inside us; (3) attract the attention of the person with whom we want contact; (4) put that person in the appropriate mood to respond to us; and (5) exchange invisible messages which can't necessarily be expressed verbally. (This final aspect – invisible messages – is obviously 'communion'.) The crucial one here is number (4): 'put the person in the appropriate mood to respond' is another way of saying, 'play your objective'. When Sonya wants to persuade Tortsov that the group is bored with the 'Money-burning' étude and don't want to do it any more, she achieves her objective by picking up on the invisible signs that Tortsov is giving out and adapting her actions accordingly. Vanya, however, is totally unsuccessful in achieving his objective when he tries to distract Tortsov from reading a letter. Inadvertently, his objective adapts (wrongly) from 'distracting Tortsov' to 'entertaining his peers'. The more they laugh, the more he is seduced into turning his attention out into the auditorium and away from his on-stage partner.

Two other vital qualities of adaptations are their 'amplitude' and 'appropriateness'. The example used by Tortsov to illustrate his point is that of a young man wanting to attract the attention of his sweetheart. According to whether she is across the street, at her window, with her mother or near a rival lover, the young man has to adapt his actions in terms of their size (amplitude) and nature (appropriateness) to express his adoration.

Added to objectives, amplitude and appropriateness is 'unexpectedness'. For all his emphasis on technical preparation and psycho-physical homework, Stanislavsky prized moments of unexpectedness on the stage. The key to unexpectedness is letting the subconscious go to work. Okay, but that's easier said than done! However, Stanislavsky proposes that, if you turn your attention from yourself and focus it fully on your partner, you will be surprised by your own intuitive adaptations. So now you know what to do to 'adapt' successfully on stage: focus on your partner and play your objective with the relevant amplitude, appropriateness and unexpectedness.

Having articulated the different qualities needed for successful adaptation, Stanislavsky spends some time in this chapter defining four different kinds of adaptation that an actor may experience: they are 'mechanical', 'motor', 'intuitive' and 'semi-conscious'. The main adaptation to be avoided is the *mechanical* one: this is a cliché or 'rubber stamp' from the vocabulary of conventional, lifeless, theatrical routine. Stanislavsky is less critical of motor adaptations. These come into being when, in rehearsals, actors make subconscious adaptations to their characterisations and then the director draws attention to these adaptations; for a while, they become conscious before eventually being subsumed back into the actors' characterisations where they then become 'motor'. Although these adaptations are no longer subconscious, the actors haven't sacrificed their sense of naturalness in performing them. 'Intuitive' adaptations are the most desirable! These usually arise when actors are wholly relaxed on stage, and engaged in an ongoing process of improvisation: this state is ideal for actors, leading to all kinds of unexpected adjustments. It is possible, however, to prompt 'semiconscious' adaptations. Tortsov illustrates this by constructing a long list of human qualities or moods; the students then select a word randomly, and pursue their objectives adapting their actions according to the quality of the word. If you already have a grasp of communion and inner improvisation, Chapter 11 is remarkably straightforward. If not, it seems a little strange, but it's worth persevering.

Stanislavsky uses the conclusion of the chapter for several purposes. At the end of their class, the students see a number of placards hung around the stage, with the following words: (1) Inner Tempo-Rhythm; (2) Inner Characterisation; (3) Control and Finish; (4) Inner Ethics and Discipline; (5) Dramatic Charm; and (6) Logic and Coherence. Displaying the placards allows Stanislavsky (via Tortsov) to link the psychological work of *An Actor Prepares* with the physical work of *Building a Character*, which contains chapters on 'Towards a Physical Characterisation', 'Restraint and Control', 'Tempo-Rhythm in Movement', 'Stage Charm' and 'Towards an Ethics for the Theatre'. The placards, therefore, serve as a reminder that the two books should be considered in tandem: it's a psycho-physical 'system', linking the inner work of *An Actor Prepares* with the physical work of *Building a Character*.

The final section of the chapter also reminds us that the three strands of (1) actor-training; (2) rehearsal processes; and (3) performance techniques are interconnected but different, and the work so far in the book has focused on the first: actor-training. The sixth placard, 'Logic and Coherence', provides Stanislavsky with an opportunity to recap the work to date, as given circumstances, 'If', physical actions, concentration of attention, and objectives and units all emphasise the need for logic and coherence in on-stage activity. By the end of Chapter 11,

Stanislavsky has stressed the importance of practical learning over theorising, as well as drawing to a close the first section of psycho-technique. What follows in the next chapter assumes that the students' inner instruments have now been prepared and warmed up to begin serious playing.

Chapter 12: 'Inner Motive Forces'

This is the shortest chapter in the book, yet in many ways the ideas within it are some of the most crucial in terms of understanding psycho-physical acting. The unfortunate result of the chapter's short-ness is that its contents may be seen as not very important. Don't be fooled – they're vital!

Tortsov begins the chapter by telling the students that their inner 'instruments' are now ready: all that remains is to find the appro-priate inner 'musicians'. So who might those 'musicians' be? The students quickly propose the 'mind' and 'feeling' as two possibilities, and then an undue amount of time is spent identifying a third. Here, Stanislavsky's storytelling device gets in the way of itself, as the students' attempts to name the third 'musician' – 'will' – seem to muddy the issue, rather than clarify its importance. Eventually, how-ever, 'Thought', 'Feeling' and 'Will' (or brain, heart and body) are labelled as the triumvirate of the 'inner motive forces' which operate within each actor (see Figure 2.3).

Part of the difficulty with this chapter is its use of terminology. 'Will' is also described as 'desire', which sets it very close to 'feeling' or 'emotion', and for a student-actor this blurring can be unhelpful. Today some Russian practitioners call 'will' the 'action-centre', which allies it very closely with the body, the vehicle for carrying out actions. And this is where we unlock a subtle shift from the early 'system' (as explored in *An Actor Prepares*) and the later practice of Active Analysis (discussed in Chapter 1, this volume, pp. 33–7). Although Stanislavsky writes that feeling, will and thought are interdependent and equal, the two sequences of acting that he describes both put 'will' at the end of the chain. The first sequence he proposes is that the actors' *mental* understanding of the playtext arouses their *emotions* which then prompt their *will* into action. The second sequence is that the actors' *emotional* reaction to the playtext arouses their *mind* which then prompts their *will* into action. In other words, Stanislavsky didn't yet consider 'will' as an initiating force in its own right. By the time he came to work on Active Analysis, his thoughts had completely changed, and he understood that sometimes the will – or body – could in fact form the first link in the chain.

This chapter is tantalisingly elusive. Tortsov says that he can't yet discuss the inner motive forces in detail with his students as they still have a certain amount of preparation to do before they will fully understand the process. Unfortunately, this doesn't help the reader of *An Actor Prepares*, who isn't necessarily engaged in the lengthy actor-training that the fictional students are. Thus, to some extent Stanislavsky undermines the value of his own chapter. Certainly, the inner motive forces are often underemphasised in contemporary actor-training, when in fact the triumvirate of body, mind and emotions lies at the heart of Stanislavsky's whole 'system'. After all, 'adaptations' involve inner dialogues between the three, 'communion' involves connecting to partners through brain, heart and body, and identifying 'objectives' is an emotional, desire-driven activity and not a purely intellectual one.

The chapter comes to an abrupt halt with Tortsov congratulating the students that their instruments are ready and the musicians identified, so now the real work can begin. In many ways, Chapter 12 is a compromise. Stanislavsky needed to discuss the communication between the inner motive forces and yet the language he chooses is not entirely convincing. Maybe he himself was unsure of what vocabulary to use. Maybe he was aware that will or 'action' had a more significant role in actor-training and rehearsal techniques than he was giving it credit for. Maybe he simply hadn't yet formulated or understood how to implement it. That would be his later life's work with Active Analysis.

Chapter 13: 'The Unbroken Line'

Although many of the exercises have touched upon issues of performance, the main emphases so far have been on actor-training and analysis of text. The three are brought together in the short, sharp Chapter 13, when Tortsov continues his 'musician' analogy, declaring to his class that their inner instruments are 'at concert pitch!' (Stanislavsky 1980: 252). They are ready to start working towards performance.

Figure 2.3
The Inner Motive Forces,
illustrated by Russian director,
Vladimir Ananyev

THOUGHT-CENTRE
located in the Head
Nose = Thought in the Thought-centre
Eyes = Feeling in the Thought-centre
Chin = Action in the Thought-centre

FEELING-CENTRE
located in the Chest

ACTION-CENTRE
located in the Groin, Arms and Legs
Fingers and Toes = Thought in the
    Action-centre
Shoulders and Knees = Feeling in the Action-centre
Elbows and Hips = Action in the Action-centre

It is the 'unbroken line' which links inner and outer processes by means of a sequence of physical actions. That sequence has its own logic, and that logic inspires a sense of belief within the actors, which lights their imagination and ignites their emotions. To illustrate his point, Tortsov asks Vanya to recall everything he has done that day from the moment he got up until the moment he arrived at class. By going over the list of events and repeating the sequence until it is clear and artic- ulate, Tortsov highlights the way in which life consists of an integrated whole made up of individual actions, feelings and thoughts (i.e. the three 'inner motive forces'). Once Vanya has recreated the line of the past, Tortsov then asks Kostya to create the line of the future, this time projecting himself into the afternoon, supposing the details of everything that he may do. Putting the two lines together – the line of the past and the line of the future – forms *the life of the whole day*. For actors to have a sense of the continuous line of inner actions and outer activities for their characters, they need to construct an unbroken line. This involves filling in all the details omitted by the playwright between the various characters' entrances and exits, as well as during all the on-stage activity.

The unbroken line doesn't just exist in the life of the character: it has to exist in the concentration of the actor. Using one of his lighting illustrations with different spotlights, Tortsov shows the lights in the auditorium glowing brightly, while the lights on stage are sporadic and unconnected. Once more he encourages actors to harness their attention to the stage rather than leaking it out into the auditorium. Again the shortness of the chapter is deceptive, as the inherent idea is crucial.

Chapter 14: The 'Inner Creative State'

In Chapter 16, Stanislavsky declares (via Tortsov) that 'the fundamental objective of our psycho-technique is to put us in a creative state in which our subconscious will function naturally' (Stanislavsky 1980: 281). Inherent in this aim is a balance between:

NATURAL STATE – PSYCHO-TECHNIQUE – CREATIVE STATE

The natural state and the creative state are remarkably similar, and the theory is that the more sophisticated an actor's psycho-technique, the more 'naturally' the creative state will come to us on stage. Chapter 14 contains a series of handy hints regarding how to strengthen the inner creative state and, as one of the most philosophical chapters, it requires careful reading for it not to seem like pure ideology. Essentially, this chapter links 12 and 13 by proposing that the unbroken line acts as a channel for the inner motive forces; they then serve as a kind of prism. So . . . I allow the play to filter through my inner motive forces (i.e. my own personality). They gradually take on the tone, colour, shading and moods demanded by the play. The character that emerges through this filtering still consists of my own thoughts, feelings and actions, but it is marinated in the given circumstances of the script. In this way, 'the artist in the role' emerges: it is 'me' and 'the character' at one and the same time. As the actor, I am driven by certain components: the character's objectives, the movement of the play, my objects of concentration, my contact with the other characters and my own sense of artistic truthfulness. All these components Stanislavsky calls the 'elements of the inner creative mood' – or state – and their fusion accesses within actors the 'inner creative mood' – or state.

Tortsov is keen to point out that the inner creative state is a perfectly natural state in which to be. In some ways, it is *worse* than our everyday state in that it can encourage exhibitionism, and yet it can be *better* than our everyday state because of our unique contact with the audience. (In fact, the audience is a vital component in experiencing the inner creative state.) Although it is a natural state, it is actually very hard to maintain: if the actor's psycho-physical apparatus is malfunctioning because he or she has developed mechanical or lazy habits, or has only half-prepared the role, or has personal worries or ill health, the inner creative state suffers. That said, there are specific ways (recommended by Tortsov) in which the inner creative state may be established. First of all, actors have to be in *direct* contact with their on-stage partner, not the audience; they must choose objectives that they can believe in; and they need to connect absolutely with whatever their objects of attention might be. Any degree of faking it cannot coexist with the inner creative state. While this advice is quite general, and it seems as if we have heard it before, Tortsov goes on to offer a step-by-step guide to preparing the inner creative state before going on stage.

He recommends that actors arrive two hours ahead of their first entrance in a play, so that they may start 'kneading' their psycho-physical raw materials like clay. First of all, they should free their muscles from all physical tension. Then they should warm up their imaginations by choosing an object and allowing various fantasies to unravel. They should then work through the circles of attention, from a very small circle close to themselves to an enormous one taking in the whole auditorium. Finally, the actors should think of an objective, and motivate it, then change it, then add others, and keep changing the imaginative fiction, ensuring that they always *believe* in their physical actions. In this way, they can warm up their imaginations, their bodies, and the interdepending 'brothers' of psychology and physicality. A testing warm-up, but . . . comprehensive!

Possibly one of the most surprising elements of this chapter is how many references appear to the 'soul' and 'spirituality'. Throughout *An Actor Prepares*, there are over fifty of these references, dispelling the belief that Stanislavsky's 'system' was either dry and intellectual, or emotional and psychotic. It is, in fact, extremely holistic, combining body, thought and emotion with the more intangible elements of 'energy' or 'spirituality'. Given the Soviet reluctance to express esoteric ideas, it is surprising that so many appear in the English trans-lation. It shouldn't be forgotten, though, that underlying the inner creative state is the character's rock-solid 'objective'. When Tortsov suggests to Vanya that he search for an imaginary slip of blue paper, he illustrates that even the most simple of objectives, executed truthfully and with a sense of faith, can ignite the inner creative state. The power and endurance of that state is in direct proportion to the coherence and significance of the objective. So, if an objective is clear-cut and defi-nite, the state will be solid and correct; if the objective is vague and indefinite, the inner creative state will be fragile. Coming towards the end of his psycho-technique, Tortsov harnesses all the elements of actor-training (along with some textual analysis) and forms an equation between a psychological state and a motivating objective. The stronger the one, the stronger the other. Given its significance, it is hardly surprising that the penultimate chapter of *An Actor Prepares* is devoted to finding the ultimate objective: the 'super-objective'.

Chapter 15: 'The Super-objective'

The 'super-objective' is the final component in Stanislavsky's 'system', although a reading of this chapter alone won't give you an absolute idea of what it is, despite its obvious importance. Tortsov begins by referring it to the *playwright*, in particular to Chekhov. (This is a little dubious, given that Chekhov felt Stanislavsky didn't really understand what his plays were about.) Then Tortsov relates it to the *plot* of a play, arguing that the greater the work, the more magnetic the super-objective will be. However, when he starts to explain it, the examples that he chooses are in relation to the *main character* in the play. So, for example, the super-objective in *Le Malade Imaginaire* is labelled from the perspective of the main male character as: 'I wish to be thought to be sick'. Bearing in mind that defining the super-objective can influence the genre of a play, even swinging it from comedy to tragedy or vice versa, it is problematic that Stanislavsky uses leading male characters (particularly ones that he himself played) to determine a whole play's super-objective.

It is not surprising then that international scholars differ in their interpretation of 'super-objectives'. On the one hand, Jean Benedetti connects it with the play as a whole (1994: 42) and Sonia Moore describes it as the actor's obligation to 'transmit to the public the author's main idea' (1984: 49). On the other hand, Sharon Carnicke describes it as 'an overriding action that links together actions throughout the play' (1998: 181) and Mel Gordon writes that an actor's super-objective and through-action 'refer to his larger or overriding goal and Action in a play' (1987: 240). There is clearly some deliberation about whether a super-objective refers to the playwright's main reason for writing the play, or the overarching concern of each actor. The confusion seems inherent in Stanislavsky himself, who – in *Creating a Role* – defines the super-objective as:

> the inner essence, the all-embracing goal, the objective of all objectives, the concentration of the entire score of the role, of all its major and minor units. The superobjective contains the meaning, the inner sense, of all the subordinate objectives of the play. In carrying out this one superobjective you have arrived at something even more important, superconscious, ineffable, which is the spirit of [the writer] himself, the thing that inspired him to write, and which inspires an actor to act.

(Stanislavsky 2000b: 78)

This definition encompasses 'all the thousands of separate, frag-mentary objectives, units, actions in a role' (ibid.: 79), as well as the kind of creative driving force that inspires writers to write and actors to act: it's specific and it's universal. It's the writer's and the actor's simultaneously. It's confusing!

In the final Chapter 16, Stanislavsky is much clearer about a number of key qualities required of a super-objective. First of all, it must support the author's point of view (in other words, each character's super-objective must have at its heart the play's main theme or preoc-cupation). Then it must excite the actor's inner motive forces: therefore, it must arise from actors working it through creatively without being too intellectual. Perhaps the most striking idea is that the super-objective must unite actor, director and playwright: it cannot be superimposed by the director, but must arise out of the cast's collec-tive understanding of a play. Only then will each actor be aroused by his or her chosen super-objective, while simultaneously serving or reflecting the playwright's intention in writing the play. It is the director's job to help the actors ask the right questions and hunt out the right details to identify their super-objectives satisfyingly and 'accu-rately'. Once you start considering all these elements ('it can't be imposed, it must unite actor with playwright, it must move the actors to want to execute it'), you realise how difficult it is to identify a super-objective. And yet it is hugely important to get it right, as it has the potential to create real live drama on the stage, with actors genuinely listening and responding to each other.

Despite the complexities, some very useful points are clarified in Chapter 15, not the least of which is Stanislavsky's definition of the 'sys-tem's' three key linchpins: (1) inner grasp; (2) the through line of action; and (3) the super-objective. Here, 'inner grasp' seems to refer as much to the play having a grasp over the actors and the actors having a grasp on the play, as to the 'grasp' defined in Chapter 10 'Communion' as the connection between the actors themselves. As for the 'through line of action', this is described explicitly in Chapter 16 as being a series of large objectives within which the small objectives are subsumed, as the actor heads straight for the super-objective. The smaller objectives form the undercurrent of actions driving the through line forward, with the signposts of larger objectives showing the actor the way. The 'through line of action' differs from the 'unbroken line' of the previous chapter, in that it is as much to do with the *play's structure* (galvanising all the smaller 'units' and 'objectives'), as it is with the *actors' on-stage attention*. Along with the 'super-objective', 'the through line of action' forms 'the creative base of the system as a whole' (Stanislavsky 1980: 275).

In the twenty-first century, there are positives and negatives regarding Stanislavsky's heavy emphasis on the super-objective, not least of which is the absence of an absolute definition. The negative aspect arises when we consider postmodern drama, where the importance of linear narrative is significantly reduced. A more chaotic, haphazard approach to dramatic structure exists nowadays, in which the idea of an overarching, harmonising backbone is irrelevant. There needn't be a common journey that the director or playwright want the audience to take. Spectators are often expected to respond to a performance moment by moment, according to whatever images or text are presented to them in an apparently random order. That said, there are positive aspects to the super-objective. The main one is that it encourages performers to abandon any extraneous detail and head straight for the main desire (i.e. the super-objective). By doing so, actors paradoxically have a much greater freedom and sense of inner improvisation. They know where they are heading, they know the course, therefore they can be bold in each moment and respond to the adaptations that arise unexpectedly. If we take a broad overview, Stanislavsky seems to be suggesting that actors' preparation should begin with detailed analysis, so that the super-objective can be carefully identified. However, once it has been identified, the performers are then free to let the detailed preparation fall away, like the supports from a rocket launch, so that they can play 'in the moment' with the super-objective as the steering shaft.

Regardless of the various complexities and discrepancies, Tortsov is clear by the end of the chapter that his students are now equipped with the essential components of his 'system'. He can't promise that the 'system' will manufacture inspiration, but it should prepare the ground for it. The elusive nature of inspiration occupies the last chapter of *An Actor Prepares*.

Chapter 16: 'On the Threshold of the Subconscious'

The final chapter is inevitably problematic as Stanislavsky tries to rationalise processes that are essentially sensate. As he himself (via Tortsov)

Figure 2.4 Stanislavsky as Astrov in Chekhov's *Uncle Vanya* (1899)

acknowledges, the realm of the subconscious is something that actors have to experience themselves and they can't necessarily learn about it through any theoretical means. Yet the technical 'grammar' that he has devised through his 'system' is geared towards the 'poetry' of an actor's spontaneous creativity; therefore, it is important that the book concludes with a chapter addressing the subconscious, however esoteric it may be.

Chapter 16 begins with an overview of the steps taken so far towards the threshold of the subconscious: the actors' inner preparation (Step 1) leads to the development of the inner creative state (Step 2), in which they seek out a play's super-objective (Step 3) and their own through lines of action (Step 4). Following this sequence, conscious technique leads to the region of subconscious inspiration. This all sounds mightily impossible – but actually it can be accessed through the most ridiculous of unexpected moments. Stanislavsky suggests that, when accidental events occur during performances, the actors' subconscious takes over and starts creating in exciting and unexpected ways. These events can be terribly simple, such as a prop falling on the floor or other actors forgetting their lines. Many performers are terrified of these moments; yet Tortsov suggests that they are incredibly useful and rich for actors, and as such they should be exploited to the full.

Of course, the frustration is that these unexpected moments cannot be predicted, and any subconscious activity inevitably becomes conscious once you start thinking about it. So, Tortsov offers various conscious steps to try and activate the work of the subconscious. Using the Money-burning étude, he invites Kostya to 'enter a creative state'. The sequence that Kostya has to follow is (1) to note any physical and mental tension; (2) to relax his muscles so that his body is ready for work; (3) to transfer this relaxation to the imagination and the given circumstances of the play so that his mind is ready for flights of fantasy; (4) to justify this feeling of relaxation by focusing on an objective; (5) to add new suppositions and objectives that appeal to his imagination; and (6) to allow these new suppositions to arouse real emotions. Again, on paper it sounds all too easy – and an adventurous actor just has to get up and try it. Nonetheless, the combination of relaxation, imagination, a sense of truth regarding inner actions and the actor's faith in those actions, should arouse a sense of 'I am', at which point the actor imperceptibly merges with the character (see Figure 2.4).

The vital component in this magical sequence is the imagination, as it is very closely connected with conscious mental processes and, so, it should be quite easy for us to stimulate it directly. That being the case, Stanislavsky's implication is that we should get to know ourselves and our own imaginations as thoroughly as possible to discover what images we respond to and how those images can activate our inner motive forces of thought, feeling and will.

And yet. . . . Imagination is only one of the elements of the inner creative state on Stanislavsky's list, which also includes desires and objectives, emotions, a sense of truth and a sense of faith. To tickle the subconscious, we need only take one of these components, and then, according to Stanislavsky, push it to its limit. This is an important instruction, because 'when your conscious psycho-technique is carried *to its fullest extent* the ground is prepared for nature's subconscious process' (Stanislavsky 1980: 293; my emphasis). Throughout the chapter, Stanislavsky reiterates that even the smallest action, sensation or technical exercise should be 'pushed to its limit of possibility, to the boundary of human *truth, faith* and the sense of "I am"' (ibid.). And pushing to the limits is about being brave. It's about accommodating the obstacles that inevitably arise when we're working with the subconscious. The major obstacle, of course, is that, as actors, we have to create our masterpieces in front of our audience's very eyes. But there are other obstacles that we create for ourselves, such as being vague in the choices we make about our characters, as well as trying to play parts for which we're simply not suitable. Perhaps the most surprising obstacle that Stanislavsky lists is 'being too conscientious' – making too much effort. Throughout *An Actor Prepares*, the words 'simple', 'simplicity' and 'cut ninety-five per cent' abound. For all the hard work that Stanislavsky expected of his students, he also wanted them to eliminate extraneous detail and unnecessary effort: they had to have fun when creating their characters.

We're reminded in this final chapter that the principal aids to subconscious work are the 'super-objective' and the 'through line of action'. Stanislavsky still doesn't offer a neat little formula for identifying these tools. Yet, at the same time, he frustratingly suggests that the super-objective is the key to subconscious creativity. The chapter's final message, however, is very clear: technique alone cannot access inspiration, yet, combined with imagination, belief and truth, it forms a firm foundation for an actor's craftsmanship.

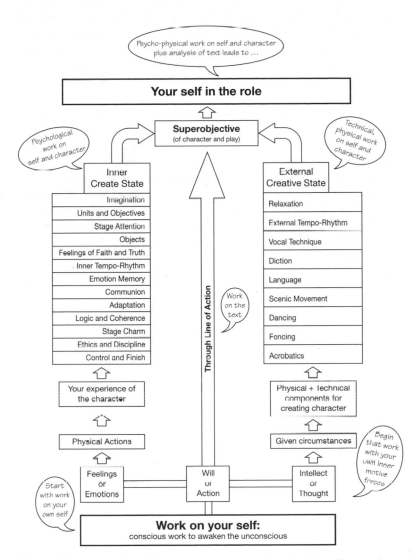

Figure 2.5 An overview of Stanislavsky's 'system' (adapted from Benedetti (1994: 61) and Lewis (1986))

The closing chapter of *An Actor Prepares* is rich in epigrams and advice. Underlying that advice are ideas that would later inform the Method of Physical Actions and Active Analysis. The intention of Stanislavsky's proposed artistic process was to lead the actor to '*the conception and birth of a new being – the person in the part*' (Stanislavsky 1980: 312). In negotiating this process, Stanislavsky tried to elide his actors' technical craft with their natural, human behaviour. Nature and natural behaviour are referred to throughout *An Actor Prepares*, and it comes as no surprise that the final words are concerned with natural laws. For those of us to whom the book seems either too esoteric on the one hand or too analytical on the other, the closing references remind us that in this – the first book of the trilogy – Stanislavsky simply tried to find words, exercises and images that connected young actors with their own instinctive responses. Once they were aware of those processes, they could begin to replace the phoney staginess of early twentieth-century acting with a craft based on theatrical truth and natural behaviour (see Figure 2.5).

DESCRIPTION AND ANALYSIS OF *THE SEAGULL*

INTRODUCTION

Revolutionary endeavours are often the result of chance rather than intention and, in many respects, this was the case with the Moscow Art Theatre's first presentation of *The Seagull* in 1898. When all the components are considered together, it seems remarkable that the production became such a high point of modern theatre history, especially since the only person with any faith in the project was Nemirovich-Danchenko. So, what was it about the production that now renders it a fascinating example of Stanislavsky's theories in practice?

In the course of the following chapter, we shall see where the seeds of many principles explored in *An Actor Prepares* (and later in the Method of Physical Actions and Active Analysis) first took root. What also emerges is that, curiously, Stanislavsky often felt he had no idea what he was doing. Yet a detailed study of his 'production plan' reveals why *The Seagull* became so significant, as Stanislavsky smashed existing rehearsal practices and revolutionised methods of theatre-making.

THE SEAGULL'S FLIGHT PATH

NEMIROVICH-DANCHENKO'S INFLUENCE

Although the 'plan' of *The Seagull* was undeniably insightful, it is quite possible that Stanislavsky would never have chosen the play, had it not been for the literary taste and understanding of Vladimir Nemirovich-Danchenko. To appreciate his influence, let's return to the night of 22 June 1897 and the haunts of the Slavyansky Bazaar. . . .

It was Nemirovich who initiated the eighteen-hour meeting, driven by his thoughts on actor-training as he taught it at the Philharmonic School. Besides encouraging his student-performers to be daring, fascinating and confident, he wanted them to be aware of relevant social issues, as well as the psychological development of dramatic characters and how to merge the actor's craft with the playwright's voice. These were issues about which he felt so passionate that he had to share them with Stanislavsky on that night in June. However, actor-training wasn't their only preoccupation. In the course of the Slavyansky encounter, the two men discussed their desire for theatre to be collaborative, believing that all the roles in a play, however small, must be treated with the appropriate 'creative attitude'. So, late into the night, their discussion threw up ideas of an ensemble-driven theatre, the kind that would later prove vital for getting inside Chekhov's unconventional writing.

Possibly the greatest influence exerted by Nemirovich at the Slavyansky meeting was on the repertoire. While Stanislavsky was an ardent admirer of comedies and classics, Nemirovich argued vehemently that new writing should form the kernel of their pioneering enterprise. He was attracted by daring, and he recognised in *The Seagull* a play that abolished the normal rules of dramatic form. However, he didn't just have to convince the rather inexperienced Stanislavsky to appreciate the play's merits, he also had to persuade the writer to surrender it up to the infant company in the first place. He knew that Chekhov would be reticent and that a compelling sales pitch was needed, so Nemirovich wrote to the playwright, declaring:

> Only a literary man with taste would know how to present your plays, a man who knows how to appreciate the beauties of your works and who is, at the same time, an expert producer himself. Such a man I can truthfully claim to be.
>
> (Nemirovich cited in Balukhaty 1952: 50–1)

Nemirovich's 'pitch' continued, exclaiming that this was the only modern play and Chekhov the only living writer 'to be of any interest to a theatre with a model repertoire' (ibid.: 52). Perhaps the deal-clincher for Chekhov was Nemirovich's astute awareness that there was something special in the author's writing, something that demanded 'bridges' over which the producer must lead the audience to help them understand the images conjured up. Without these 'bridges', the play would simply fall into the 'crude conventions' so popular with the late nineteenth-century theatre-goer. In other words, Nemirovich knew the play was a challenge to the spectator – it was no easy watch, and that was what made it exciting and attractive to him as a producer. It may well have been his awareness of this that twisted Chekhov's arm.

Once he had convinced Chekhov to hand over *The Seagull* to the Moscow Art Theatre, Nemirovich then had to elucidate its many qualities to Stanislavsky, who in the meantime was struggling hard to comprehend the play. The first stage in mounting the 1898 production involved Nemirovich patiently unlocking for Stanislavsky the reverberations and complexities of the writing. It would then be Stanislavsky's task to convert those essentially literary ideas into appropriate stage pictures. The early discussions weren't easy and, over the course of many evenings, Nemirovich 'hammered all the beauties of Chekhov's work' into Stanislavsky's head (Stanislavsky 1982: 321). Thereafter, Stanislavsky travelled to the Ukraine to come up with his detailed production plan. Thus, the staging of *The Seagull* was a complete team effort: without Nemirovich, Stanislavsky probably would have avoided the play. Without Stanislavsky's vivid imagination and understanding of stage pictures, the Moscow Art Theatre might never have found its 'house style' (a style which was to define its international identity – even to the extent of adopting a seagull as a logo). And without the Moscow Art Theatre, Chekhov might have disappeared into theatrical obscurity. This serendipitous meeting of minds might explain why *The Seagull* hadn't successfully taken flight before. After all, 1898 was not the first year in which the play was staged.

THE ALEKSANDRINSKY 'DUCK'

The year 1897 had seen the premiere of *The Seagull* at the Aleksandrinsky Theatre in St Petersburg. The first night proved to be disastrous, although following performances gained in success. Under the direction of Yevtikhy Karpov, the rehearsal schedule included one read-through, five half-day rehearsals and two dress rehearsals: unbelievable under any circumstances, let alone the production of a daunting new play like *The Seagull*. Karpov's production copy shows a scattering of stage directions, such as 'Trigorin walks to the back of the stage, then comes out to the front from left' (cited in Balukhaty 1952: 25), and mentions several props, including cigarettes, matches and a few wood shavings. A handful of sketches indicate certain positionings for the actors. But that's about it! Chekhov was due to turn up to the first rehearsal, but failed to show, leaving the initial reading of the script to the poor stage manager, with the result that the actors had no means of penetrating the play's haunting 'half-tones'. They couldn't understand how their personal *emplois* fitted into the style, as proven by the fact that the leading actress, Maria Savina, changed from Nina to Arkadina to Masha, before pulling out of the production entirely – all within eight rehearsals!

The first-night audience arrived expecting their favourite comedienne, Elizaveta Levkeyeva, to be presenting them with a rip-roaring comedy. Instead, they were left baffled and confused by the opening act with the character Konstantin Trepliov's 'symbolist' play, leading to cat-calls and whoops of disappointment. An account of the second night gives some indication of what the first night must have been like:

> what made all the difference and what distinguished the second performance from the first was that the actors had learnt their parts. They did not mouth their speeches any more, and that was why everybody got quite a different impression of the play.
>
> (Tychinsky cited in Balukhaty 1952: 30)

In a letter to Chekhov, Nemirovich recalls the words of a friend, who had seen the fourth performance, saying that 'the play could not possibly have succeeded in view of such an incredibly bad performance by the cast and such an utter lack of understanding of the characters and their moods' (Nemirovich cited in ibid.: 31). The reviews endorsed the comments of the audience, declaring that 'The play is impossibly bad' and that 'From all points of view, whether of idea, literature or stage, Chekhov's play cannot even be called bad, but absolutely absurd' (Nemirovich-Danchenko 1937: 65). All this goes to prove just how great was the challenge that lay before Stanislavsky in preparing his production plan and, in retrospect, how extraordinary was the collective achievement of Chekhov, Nemirovich and Stanislavsky in producing the final result.

THE SEAGULL FLIES

STANISLAVSKY'S METHOD

Stanislavsky's first reaction to the play was one of complete incomprehension. He himself admitted that, as soon as he was left alone with the script, he felt bored! Yet little by little as he sat in his brother's study in Kharkov, he fell under the play's spell. His reaction was entirely instinctive, as – intellectually – he could hardly grasp what the play was about. Maybe the very fact that he didn't have an intellectual grasp enabled him to operate on a deeper, more intuitive level, and he began to experience the life of *The Seagull* with his 'inner eye and ear' (Stanislavsky cited in Balukhaty 1952: 54). The resulting production plan left Nemirovich amazed at Stanislavsky's fiery and highly gifted imagination. As Stanislavsky completed the plan of each scene, he sent it to Nemirovich, who began the initial rehearsal with a four-hour discussion of the first two acts. He then passed on to the actors the gestures, movements, rhythmic choices and interpretations made by Stanislavsky (and tweaked by himself). Of the twenty-six rehearsals, Nemirovich led fifteen and Stanislavsky nine; including three dress rehearsals, a total of eighty hours was spent rehearsing *The Seagull* with all its nuances and textures.

ACT 1

The first impressions

Stanislavsky's production plan looks very much like a traditional prompt copy, in the sense that the script appears on the left, with numerically ordered notes on the right-hand page indicating where and how the characters move and talk. Accompanying the notes are a myriad of sketches. Perhaps one of the most striking features of the first page is the highly detailed ground plan of the set for Act 1 (see Figure 3.1). Hot-houses, a lake, a stream, a bridge, bushes and sunflowers mark out the landscape, along with various paths and trees. A rocking bench is placed directly at the front of the stage, signalling that, at some point, the actors will break a major theatrical convention and sit with their backs to the audience, as indeed they do during Konstantin's play. Although the detail of the ground plan is startling enough in itself, its sense of perspective is fascinating: as spectators, we are invited to feel that what we see on the stage is only a 'slice' of the life that actually exists in the play. We are encouraged to imagine that, when the actors exit the scene, they don't return to their dressing rooms to sip coffee and smoke cigarettes, but, rather, they continue the lives of their characters beyond the boundaries of the stage. In other words, a highly elaborate invitation to 'realism' is presented to the audience simply from the first visual image of the set.

Then once we start reading the production plan, we discover that, even before the curtain is raised, a whole atmospheric (almost cinematic) lighting and soundscape has been designed to conjure up the play's inner life:

> The dim light of a lantern on top of a lamp-post, distant sounds of a drunkard's song, distant howling of a dog, the croaking of frogs, the crake of a landrail, the slow tolling of a distant church-bell – help the audience to get the feel of the sad monotonous life of the characters. Flashes of lightning, faint rumbling of *thunder* in the distance. After the raising of the curtain a pause of ten seconds.
> (Stanislavsky cited in Balukhaty 1952: 139)

As we discussed in Chapter 2, Stanislavsky has often been accused of inviting actors to ignore their audiences, and to focus all their attention behind the imaginary fourth wall. Yet straight away in the production plan, we see that he wants to weave a spell over the audience, through their senses as well as their intellects. The fact that he requires a ten-second pause once the curtain has been raised indicates his desire to create a sense of suspense, as if we should count the seconds between the flash of lightning and the crash of thunder to see how close the storm is coming. The use of 'pathetic fallacy' (whereby the weather reflects the inner life of characters) is prevalent throughout the production plan, adding to the subtle layers upon which the play operates. The ten-second pause as the curtain rises would also have given the original spectators a chance to absorb the details of a set that Stanislavsky knew would challenge their usual expectations of painted canvases.

Masha and Medvedenko

Stanislavsky's understanding of psycho-physical behaviour is immediately revealed with the arrival of the first two characters – Masha and

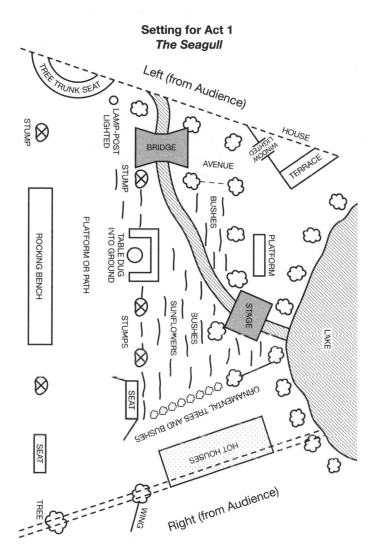

Figure 3.1 Ground plan of Act 1 of *The Seagull*, adapted from Stanislavsky 1938: 118

the schoolteacher, Medvedenko. Throughout the play, Masha is seen to be earthy and noisy: she does solid physical things. She slurps her tea loudly, she sniffs snuff and, here, she cracks nuts. As we shall see, her noisy behaviour is often placed at exactly the point where she can gain attention, or 'pull focus'. She is a needy character, in an environment where there are far more interesting and beautiful females whose needs will be served more swiftly. Medvedenko smokes heavily during the whole play. In other words, he surrounds himself in a cloud of impenetrable dinge, preventing himself from seeing what is really going on in front of his very nose with Masha and her affections. By giving actors simple physical activities, Stanislavsky is able to touch upon deeper psychological implications. Although the audience may not consciously pick up on the reverberations, he has provided his actors with wonderful nuances with which to inform their characterisations.

Perpetuating the illusion that the life of the characters goes beyond the confines of the stage, Stanislavsky ignores Chekhov's stage direction that Masha and Medvedenko sit down (Chekhov 1990: 1). Instead, he uses their two-page dialogue to zigzag on and off the stage, as if they are taking an after-dinner walk. These aren't two characters who have come here to present a piece of dialogue to an eagerly attentive audience: instead, we as spectators are encouraged to feel as if we are eavesdropping on a conversation that is taking place almost casually. Stanislavsky breaks their dialogue into sections as they exit the stage and return, rather like a pendulum. This gives us the sense of life passing in its usual way, but also that this life is fateful – its course is unalterable; what happens between Masha and Medvedenko is inevitable. In the brief pause in their dialogue (specified by Chekhov, ibid.: 2), during which they momentarily exit, the hammering of the workmen grows louder. Once more, the soundscape is used to create a sense of tension, of imminent foreboding.

Enter Sorin and Konstantin

Realism leaps to the fore with the arrival of Konstantin (Kostya) and Sorin. Where Chekhov has '*Enter right*, SORIN *and* KONSTANTIN' (ibid.), Stanislavsky describes how they 'walk through some bushes on to the path, pushing the branches out of their way, bending down, climbing over garden seats' (Stanislavsky cited in Balukhaty 1952: 141).

Instantly we have a sense that we are in a part of the garden not used very often. There is a feeling of awkwardness, and even of subterfuge when, some lines later, Masha and Medvedenko 'emerge from behind a bush' (ibid.). Maybe all will not be what it seems. . . .

The combination of Masha, Medvedenko, Sorin and Konstantin sets up a fascinating cobweb of **tempo-rhythms**. When Konstantin requests that they leave: 'Medvedenko begins to walk away obediently. Masha remains standing, deep in thought. Sorin sits down on the rocking bench, swaying up and down' (ibid.: 143). This juxtaposition of images illustrates Stanislavsky's musicality – in terms of rhythm and stage pictures. At the same time, it reveals his intuitive understanding of what he would later call in *An Actor Prepares* the 'inner motive forces': thought, feeling and action (see Chapter 2, pp. 69–70). Medvedenko has a linear path: he is action-orientated. He does what he is told: his sense of etiquette and manners is acute. Masha has no path at all: she is static. Her thought-centre governs her at this moment. Sorin strikes up a miniature pendulum motion, not dissimilar to the bigger pendulum created by Masha and Medvedenko walking from one side of the stage to the other. Sorin's path has movement, but goes nowhere, just like his whole life. We discover during the course of the play that he has big dreams and desires, but no longer the physical stamina to activate them. In the middle of these three constrained tempo-rhythms, we see Konstantin, utterly driven by his over-stimulated emotion-centre. Masha is torn between two lovers – the methodical, action-based schoolteacher and the imaginative, emotion-based writer. But she knows with whom her destiny lies: as if 'awakening from a reverie' (Stanislavsky cited in Balukhaty 1952: 143) she follows Medvedenko out.

A complex dialogue!

The dialogue between Sorin and Kostya is very complex, as it involves working with a prop, inner actions versus outer activities, inner/outer tempo-rhythms, central and peripheral actions, and tiny details versus the bigger picture. Let's unpack all these.

Props were an important part of Stanislavsky's growing awareness of psycho-physicality, so it is not by chance that Konstantin arrives carrying a bundle containing Nina's outfit for his play. The relationship between an actor and a prop can access deep psychological information and add unconscious layers to the spectators' perception of events.

There is an intimacy evoked by Konstantin handling Nina's costume, as well as establishing him as the director of his play. He is forming and shaping not only her performance but also the experience that he wants his audience (particularly his mother and her writer-lover) to undergo. The image becomes startlingly clear when, some time later in Act 1, Nina arrives and Konstantin 'starts unfolding Nina's costume. . . . During this scene, Nina undoes her hair and drapes herself in a sheet. Konstantin is assisting her, pinning her stage costume for her here and there' (ibid.: 153). There is a naive eroticism attached to them mutually preparing her to be exhibited before the man (Trigorin) who ends up becoming her lover. Certainly, when Stanislavsky eventually sets up the scene for Konstantin's play, there is a significant sense of sexual awareness, as the prop evolves from inanimate bundle to revealing adornment: '[Nina] is draped in a white sheet, her hair hangs loosely down her back, the sheet, as it falls down her arms, forms something that resembles a pair of wings, through which Nina's bust and arms are faintly outlined' (ibid.: 159). Here, with Sorin, however, the prop is used to reveal the underlying tension. Konstantin tries to balance the bundle against the side of the table and, on failing, throws it down on the ground. His action is performed without comment as an accompaniment to the dialogue, and yet, through the bundle's 'lack of cooperation', we see Konstantin's frustration that he can't control Nina. And she's late! The physical activity reverberates with psychological metaphor. There is a similar effect with the rocking bench: Sorin constantly tries to stabilise it, while Konstantin unsettles it every time he leaps up and down.

The contradiction between inner action and outer activity is cleverly encapsulated in Stanislavsky's stage directions for Konstantin's long speeches that rail against his mother and art. Stanislavsky specifies that Konstantin remains lying on the bench for the duration of the dialogue. He then juxtaposes the stillness of the posture with sudden outbursts of excitability – Kostya puffs a cigarette, shakes off the ash, tears up flowers and grass-stalks, abruptly sits up and then lies down again. This sequence reveals the conflict within Kostya's inner motive forces: by lying still, his body (action-centre) is trying to contain the explosiveness of his emotion- and thought-centres, which every so often get the better of him through these abrupt physical actions. It is all very clever, as a dynamic tension is created between Kostya's inner and outer tempo-rhythms. Added to this, Kostya's actions become more *central*, as he becomes more agitated. In other words, the tearing of the flower or the shaking of ash are actions at the *periphery* of his body, whereas 'slapping his leg nervously' and 'beating his breast in agitation' (ibid.: 147) reveal how his intensifying frustration becomes directed towards himself rather than the physical objects around him.

With regard to visual pictures, Stanislavsky develops the tension between inner feeling and outer expression in the changing spatial relationships between Sorin and Kostya. At the start of the dialogue, Kostya lies on the bench with his head in his hand: it is casual and devil-may-care. As the tension rises, he changes to sit looking out front, before the final – more confessional or confrontational – posture in which he straddles the bench face to face with Sorin. Throughout these changing images, Sorin remains grounded and still: he yawns, hums and whistles – his tempo-rhythm is legato. Konstantin paces, smokes and tears things – his tempo-rhythm is staccato. There is a musicality in the stage-pictures as a whole and in the individual gestures of the two characters. A moment of comedy is reached at the end of the dialogue, when Nina arrives, Kostya leaps up from the bench and Sorin almost falls off, having clung on for dear life throughout the exchange. As Kostya loses his emotional balance, Sorin almost loses his physical balance.

Dancing and music

The arrival of Nina is illustrated in Stanislavsky's production plan with a flurry of small drawings, as Nina, Sorin and Kostya almost dance around each other – age and ill health encounter youth and hopeful love (see Figure 3.2). Following Sorin's departure, the text between Kostya and Nina is quite sparse – leading, of course, to the kiss lasting 'five seconds' (ibid.: 153). Littered around this dialogue are numerous stage directions with specific details for almost every line and pause: this is clearly an early kind of a Method of Physical Actions. Twice Kostya seizes Nina's hand, twice she pulls it away, the second time 'running off rapidly' (ibid.) to sit elsewhere. Taken as a whole, the stage picture consists of Konstantin trying to tie Nina down with kisses, while she constantly flies away – like a seagull? Their objectives vividly contradict each other, creating – as a result – exciting, detailed action.

By contrast, the exchange between Dorn and Polina, which follows Kostya and Nina's encounter, has very few directions. It is the same in Act 2, when Trigorin has his long speeches to Nina about playwriting.

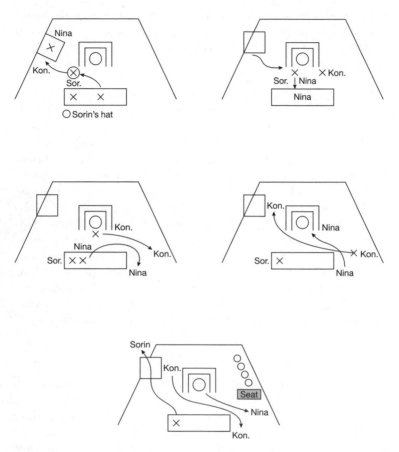

Figure 3.2 The arrival of Nina in Act 1 of *The Seagull*, adapted from
Stanislavsky's sketches (1938: 135–6). Note the dance-like movements
between Konstantin and Nina, with Sorin and his hat remaining at the
Down-Stage-Centre bench until the last moment

This may be because Stanislavsky was going to play Dorn at one point
and then he took the part of Trigorin. Perhaps he considered it unnecessary to give himself stage directions. The ensemble interactions
surrounding Konstantin's play, however, are extremely detailed,
revealing Stanislavsky's great understanding of how the musicality of

the collective voices could be drawn out. Nowhere is this more clearly seen than with the estate manager, Shamrayev, who is evidently the 'bass' instrument. Inspired by Shamrayev's tale of the famous singer, Silva, Stanislavsky creates a repeating motif, a kind of psychological gesture for the actor to integrate into his characterisation. Shamrayev becomes a bassoon-like buffoon, who, at inappropriate moments, honks the bass notes. One example follows the collapse of Kostya's play, when ethereal singing is heard across the lake. In the pause during which the other characters listen, somewhat haunted, Shamrayev leaps on a tree stump and starts conducting. Cleverly, Stanislavsky allows a moment of melancholy stillness – obviously intended by Chekhov, who inserted a pause (Chekhov 1990: 14) – but he instantly undercuts the latent sentimentality with the brusque humour of the estate manager.

Soundscapes

The moment of the singing also introduces another vital component into the production plan, again prefiguring filmic devices: that of under-scoring the action with soundscapes. This effect not only creates atmosphere but also takes the spectator on a particular emotional journey. In the middle of Kostya's play, the distant tolling of a church bell sounds. At this stage, it provokes a sense of foreboding, as well as reminding us of a world beyond the garden of Arkadina's estate (as does the singing across the lake). When the same bell is sounded during Nina's return visit in Act 4, we are flung back to this moment in Act 1 and reminded of the inevitability of Nina's sorry plight.

Sound effects are even more imaginatively created through the counterpoint of characters' voices and preoccupations. Shamrayev's crassness in telling the story of Silva, accompanied by his coarse laugh-ter, clashes with the delicacy of emotions exchanged between Nina, Trigorin and Arkadina. The 'musical score' suggested by Stanislavsky is highly expressive:

> No one laughs, Shamrayev, on the other hand, bursts out laughing even louder, then stops abruptly, repeats once more, 'Bravo, Silva!' and falls silent as suddenly as he began. A pause of fifteen seconds. No one stirs. The only sounds are the distant singing of the peasants, the croaking of the frogs and the cry of the corncrake. . . . Another pause of ten seconds.

> (Stanislavsky cited in Balukhaty 1952: 169)

This soundscape delicately takes the spectators on a subconscious exploration of circles of attention: from the bass voice of Shamrayev, to the vocal silence of each character's individual preoccupations, to the world beyond the estate and, in the final silence, back to their own preoccupations. The audience are being catapulted between the inner world (or microcosm) of the characters, and the outer world (or macrocosm) of Russia.

The closing image of the first act, which at the Art Theatre's premiere left the audience suspended in silence before bursting into tumultuous applause, is heavily cinematic in its use of soundscape. Masha's sobs at realising the futility of her love and life are cross-faded to the sound of Konstantin playing a 'frenzied waltz' (ibid.: 175) on the piano. To an almost melodramatic cacophony of sound, including the tolling of a church bell, a peasant's song, frogs, corncrakes, the knocking of the nightwatchman, 'and all sorts of other nocturnal sound effects' (ibid.: 175), the curtain falls! Whether a director today would dare to try out Stanislavsky's idea is debatable. Nonetheless, implicit in this stage direction is the creation of atmosphere: that atmosphere is as vital for the audience's emotional journey as it is for the actors' sense of realism. Although he was greatly misunderstood at the time – not least by Chekhov – Stanislavsky's exploration of sound was essentially aimed at gelling the actors and the audience into one theatrical experience in which they could all develop a sense of faith and truth.

ACT 2

Masha's tempo-rhythms

The opening stage directions for the second act are once again highly cinematic in detail, with the continuing idea of a 'pathetic fallacy' (where the weather reflects the characters' states of mind). The curtain of Kostya's makeshift stage is now 'waving in the wind and flapping against the sides of the platform' (ibid.: 179), mirroring his own tattered art and heart. Within this opening exchange, Stanislavsky has incorporated a number of physical activities for characters, which reveal their underlying tensions. Masha noisily drinks her tea throughout this scene (just as, in Act 1, she cracked nuts and, in Act 3, 'she eats noisily' (ibid.: 211)). Her noisiness serves as both a kind of attention-seeking to upstage Arkadina's reading of the Maupassant novella, and a 'naturalistic' indication of her social upbringing; after all, she is the daughter of the brusque estate manager, Shamrayev. Stanislavsky's detailed consideration of Masha's character in this scene reveals his concern for every part in the ensemble. In her short exchange with Nina about Konstantin's writing, Stanislavsky specifies precisely the changing tempo-rhythms that Masha is to use with each sentiment. She begins by speaking 'her words very rapidly and a little sharply', followed by a pause, after which she continues 'in quite a different, dreamy voice' (ibid.: 183): this betrays her deepening emotion memory as she vividly recalls Konstantin's own reading, at the same time as providing a moment of comedy when Sorin finally erupts with a snore. Although the counterpoint of Sorin and Masha is provided by Chekhov in the text, Stanislavsky carefully directs the actress playing Masha through a series of adapting tempo-rhythms to gain the maximum comic potential.

Songscapes

At several points throughout the production plan, Stanislavsky indicates that characters sing. The singing provides another texture to the sound-scape, while also operating on an emotional/psychological level. This is the case during the discussion of Sorin's health near the beginning of Act 2, when Dorn begins to hum a melody (as indeed he often does throughout the play) and Arkadina provides a harmony. This musical accompaniment to the discussion of Sorin's life suggests that the characters are avoiding their concern about his health. In other words, Stanislavsky adds layers to a scene beyond and beneath the actual words, so that the text ceases to be a conversation about Sorin's life and instead becomes a scene about others' *attitudes* to his life: their singing effortlessly expresses the **subtext**.

Physical activity versus psychological action

Dorn and Arkadina's singing is in itself a physical activity. Again, in Act 2, Stanislavsky uses physical activities to highlight characters' social status. (Don't forget that the influence of environment and heredity on psychology and social status was an important aspect of the Naturalist movement.) So, after the sipping of tea by the assembled company, Shamrayev arrives and continues his dialogue, 'stuffing bread into his mouth and washing it down with tea' (Stanislavsky cited in Balukhaty 1952: 187). Their etiquette (notwithstanding Masha's noisy slurping) is offset by Shamrayev's brusque practicality. In fact, cups of tea are used with comic regularity to express a character's inner life. When Polina and Dorn are left alone after Arkadina's row with Shamrayev, Polina 'drinks up her cup of tea at one gulp' (ibid.: 191), as if the downing of hot liquid reflects her desire to devour Dr Dorn.

The exchange between Dorn and Polina is larded with comic frustration, endorsed by the bizarre picture of Dorn doing his gymnastic exercises. He walks up and down a plank throughout Polina's entreaties, as if balancing on a tightrope. By distracting himself from the conversation like this, he seems to behave like an annoying child, refusing to engage with the adult conversation that Polina is anxious to pursue. In other words, Stanislavsky presents their conflicting objectives (Polina's to engage Dorn, Dorn's to deflect Polina) in broad, physical pictures, where psychology and physicality are inextricably linked.

It is the constant juxtaposition of physical activity with psychological action and spoken text that marks out Stanislavsky's production plan of *The Seagull* as revolutionary and extraordinary. Even when Chekhov gives characters monologues, Stanislavsky justifies the text with a physical activity. So he takes Chekhov's stage direction that Nina gives Dorn some flowers (inciting Polina to 'tear them up and throw them on the ground' (Chekhov 1990: 26)) and creates a further 'dialogue' between the flowers and Nina. During her speech about famous actresses, 'she sorts out the flowers and makes a little bunch of them' (Stanislavsky cited in Balukhaty 1952: 193). Her action transports the monologue from a theatrical device to a conversation with herself, as, through the prop (the flowers), she 'arranges' or 'makes sense' of the situation.

An intimate style of acting

In many ways, moments such as Nina with the flowers are like cinematic close-ups. The precision of the physical activity guides the audience's eye towards very specific details. Although cinema was in its infancy at the time that Stanislavsky composed his production plan, many of his ideas illustrate the way in which he explored the same kind of intimate contact that on-screen close-ups can allow. This is absolutely clear in both exchanges that Nina has in Act 2, the first with Konstantin and the second with Trigorin. Throughout these two encounters, Stanislavsky makes references to eye contact. Having presented Nina with the dead seagull, Konstantin 'looks intently and reproachfully' at her, while she 'is unable to look him straight in the face' and, thus, 'lowers her eyes' (ibid.: 193). Eventually, she turns her back on him, thereby avoiding eye contact altogether. In sharp contrast to this encounter, Nina's relationship to Trigorin is unashamedly intimate: during the conversation, she 'gazes entranced into Trigorin's pensive eyes' (ibid.: 197). Stanislavsky even stresses that, in the course of Trigorin's long speech about his writing: 'it would be advisable for Nina not to change her position, but go on looking into Trigorin's eyes all the time with rapt expression' (ibid.). The insistence on eye contact suggests a specific kind of acting. As we have already touched upon in Chapter 1, it was quite common for actors to present most of their performance Down-Stage-Centre and directly out to the audience. This was partly because stage lighting was still fairly primitive and 'DSC' was a prime spot, and partly because the actors were then close enough to the prompter to be guided through an ill-rehearsed performance. However, Stanislavsky's directions invite an intimate style of acting, requiring what he referred to as 'limitless attention to your partner' (Stanislavsky cited in Gorchakov 1994: 318). Facial expressions change, and eye contact varies in intensity: Stanislavsky draws the audience in, so that they can watch human interaction under a microscope. Although we have now become used to such detailed acting through the media of film and television, we have to remind ourselves of how revolutionary it would have been for an audience who were accustomed to the grand gesturing and loud oratory of nineteenth-century melodrama.

Comparing the two encounters between Kostya and Nina, and Nina and Trigorin also highlights the way in which Stanislavsky explored spatial dynamics. Although the majority of illustrations in his production copy are ground plans of the stage, from time to time he embellishes his stage directions with sketches of the characters. In the first dialogue, Stanislavsky shows Konstantin with his foot on a tree stump, and between him and Nina is a shotgun, upon whose barrel he leans. (See Figure 3.3a.) So, an implement of death (the gun) is placed between them along with a dead seagull; at the same time, a status game is being played, with Kostya above Nina in terms of height. Taken as a whole, the picture is threatening, rather than tender: it certainly doesn't look like a love scene. However, according to Stanislavsky's sketches, the dynamics between Nina and Trigorin are entirely

Figure 3.3 A series of sketches revealing shifting relationships between Nina, Konstantin and Trigorin, adapted from Stanislavsky's sketches (1938: 189, 193, 195, 205):

(a) With his rifle on his knees, Konstantin surveys Nina on the bench. The dead seagull lies between them

(b) Trigorin leans against the hammock, nonchalantly, while Nina looks up at him

Figure 3.3 *(continued)*

(c) Nina sits at the feet of Trigorin with the bough of the tree cast over them

(d) They now sit – equally – on the bench, with the dead seagull between them

The differing heights of the characters convey shifting states of power and intimacy

different. At first, she sits herself in a hammock, against whose side Trigorin leans casually. (See Figure 3.3b.) Then a little later, he crosses to a seat Down-Stage-Right, and Nina sits herself on a cushion at his feet. (See Figure 3.3c.) On both occasions, he is above her in terms of height, yet each time the picture is one of fascination, interest and flirtation, not intimidation as it is with Konstantin. The fact that Stanislavsky chooses to provide sketches of these two exchanges demonstrates that he wanted these spatial and pictorial comparisons to be made by the audience, either consciously or subconsciously. The final sketch that he provides of Nina and Trigorin shows them sitting together on the bench. (See Figure 3.3d.) Now they are on equal footing: they have both understood that they are in love with each other, although between them still lies the macabre body of the dead seagull, like a fateful totem. Chekhov's intention that the seagull should be a metaphor throughout the play is embellished by Stanislavsky through positioning the characters in various spatial relations to the bird (see Figure 3.4).

The penultimate stage direction of Act 2 explores the different intentions behind the various characters' eye contact. As Arkadina 'throws a quick glance at [Nina] through her lorgnette', she leads away Trigorin, who is 'still staring at Nina' (Stanislavsky cited in Balukhaty 1952: 207). Images of eyes and seeing permeate the production plan. Who really sees what's going on? In the world of actors and writers, who can really tell truth from artifice? Undoubtedly, Stanislavsky is bravely following Chekhov's lead of combining realism with symbolism, the physical with the metaphysical. And yet he was constantly haunted by a sense of self-doubt. His final direction of Act 2 is bold in terms of its theatricality, and yet his notes to Nemirovich indicate his insecurity:

> During the final pause of ten seconds it might not be a bad idea for the curtain on the platform to start swaying violently and flapping against the platform (as a hint of what is to be mentioned in Act IV). The danger is that it might produce a rather ridiculous effect. Should we try it?

(ibid.)

On the one hand, Stanislavsky seems to know that he is challenging convention; on the other hand, he is aware of the fine line between dramatic experimentation and melodramatic device. These doubts simply reinforce the fact that *The Seagull* was successful almost in spite of itself.

Figure 3.4 Stanislavsky as Trigorin and Roksanova as Nina in the 1898
production of *The Seagull* at the Moscow Art Theatre

ACT 3

Naturalistic details

The floor plan for Act 3 instantly reveals the innovative quality of the stage design. The interior of a room is shown, complete with parrot in cage, and yet it is all presented on an angle, enhancing the feeling that we are watching a slice of life rather than a neatly prepared box set for a play. The angle of the design suggests that the house – and the characters' lives – stretch far beyond the boundaries established by the stage. In contrast to the vivid soundscapes of the first two acts, Act 3 begins with a clock ticking. During his lifetime, Stanislavsky was often ridiculed by fellow practitioners (not least of whom was Chekhov himself) for his enthusiastic love of sound effects. His argument was that, paradoxically, we can hear silence much more acutely through the use of sound: the simplicity of the clock ticking suggests the chilling calm before a storm.

These details of set and sound remind us of the Naturalist movement of which Stanislavsky was a part. As stressed already, a crucial component of Naturalism was the role that heredity and environment played in the development of an individual. At the beginning of Act 3, Stanislavsky gives Masha a simple physical gesture which links her back to Dr Dorn in Act 1. She pensively traces lines on the tablecloth with her fork, just as Dorn pensively traces with his stick on the ground throughout the fracas following Kostya's play. There is an implication in *The Seagull* that Dorn might be Masha's biological father (her heredity), and yet Shamrayev is her familial father (her environment). Therefore, juxtaposed with her quiet thoughtfulness is her brusque coarseness. During this encounter with Trigorin at the top of Act 3, Stanislavsky is thorough in the details concerning Masha's character:

> It can be seen from the way in which she fills the glasses that she is an expert at that kind of thing. . . . Does it all with assumed gaiety, with the devil-may-care air of a student. . . . One arm akimbo, like a man, clinks glasses energetically, also like a man. . . . Masha empties her glass at one gulp and has a bite of something (she eats noisily), then slaps Trigorin on the back. . . . Leaning with her elbows on the table, bends over towards Trigorin.
>
> (Stanislavsky cited in Balukhaty 1952: 211, 213)

This collection of stage directions illustrates two aspects of Stanislavsky's intentions for his production plan. Just as we saw at the top of Act 2, he was eager to give as much attention to the minor characters as to the principal roles, in order to encourage a style of ensemble acting. The second intention is the way in which he sets up a very clear relationship between the actress playing Masha and the props with which she works. The aplomb with which she fills the glass and drinks the liquid, and her physical contact with the table, give us a clear insight into her psychology and her backstory. These naturalistic details also serve to undercut any sentimentality that might lie in the text. So, for example, when Masha asks Trigorin to sign a book for her, she speaks 'while struggling into rubber goloshes and buttoning her coat' (ibid.: 213). In other words, Stanislavsky cunningly provides the actress with a vigorous, practical, physical activity while her text is poetic and imaginative. This contrast reveals the contradictions within Masha's personality: she wants to be a Nina but she has to be a Polina.

Subtexts and pauses

As Masha exits, Nina enters. Following the plan established in Act 2, the close-ups of eye contact are once again put under the microscope in her exchange with Trigorin. More interesting at this point is the use of the pause. It is believed that the term 'subtext' was introduced into theatrical vocabulary by Nemirovich Danchenko and Stanislavsky, when they were first tackling *The Seagull*. The ideal moments in which subtext can be articulated are pauses. At the point in this dialogue where Trigorin reminds Nina of the dead seagull, Chekhov has inserted a pause. As an illustration of how dramatic pauses are never just empty silences, Stanislavsky provides an extensive stage direction. After a moment's awkwardness, Nina jumps to her feet to leave the room, but Trigorin catches her hand to stop her. She stands with her back to him in silence, as Trigorin raises her caught hand to kiss it. Gently she withdraws her hand from his lips and moves to the stove, where (just like Dorn and Masha lost in thought) she traces something with her finger. This is a moment of decision for her. That tracing finger marks a resolution, as she turns quickly to Trigorin to finish her speech and immediately exit. The details piled into that one 'pause' indicate a whole sequence of conflicts *between* the two characters as well as *within* each of the two characters. Their emotions battle with their thoughts,

their desires battle with their sense of duty. The vividness of Stanislavsky's imagination has jam-packed that one moment with a com-
plexity of realistic human responses, full of varying tempo-rhythms and
life-changing decisions.

Eating lunch: a physical distraction to heighten tension

Stanislavsky's intuitive sense of musicality collides the delicacy of
Trigorin and Nina with the brassier notes of Arkadina in her conversation with Sorin. Once again, Stanislavsky changes a solemn dialogue
about Sorin's health into a piece of light naturalistic conversation by
having Arkadina eat her lunch as a backdrop to the text. The noisy
clatter of her knife and fork conflict with Sorin's tentative attempts to
find the appropriate moment to ask her about money. Their contradictory objectives create a sense of comic tension: Sorin doesn't want
to spoil her lunch, which is exactly what he knows will happen as soon
as he mentions money.

Stanislavsky's musical understanding of the conversation continues
after the moment at which Sorin dares to broach the subject. The
changes of tempo-rhythm between the characters, as well as the actual
aural accompaniment of Arkadina's eating are delightfully observed.
Arkadina stops eating, she frowns, she thinks, she plays with her knife.
She stops eating again. She shakes her head slowly. She quickly fills her
glass. She starts eating vigorously. At the point at which she 'cannot
stand it any longer, she throws down her knife (a clatter of dishes on the
table) and, like the thoroughly spoilt woman she is, bursts into tears'
(Stanislavsky cited in Balukhaty 1952: 219). She then buries her face in
a napkin and remains sitting motionless. The comedy arises from the
incongruity of her lack of interest in Sorin's health versus the emotional
response that the issue of money arouses in her. However, when Sorin's
fainting fit reveals his dreadful physical state, Stanislavsky insists that the
audience be plummeted into the seriousness of the situation to the same
degree that Arkadina is:

> This scene should be played as realistically as possible, so as to deceive the
> audience. It should be played in a way to convince the audience that Sorin is
> dying. That would greatly heighten the suspense of the audience and its
> interest in what is taking place on the stage.

(ibid.: 221)

Here we see Stanislavsky playing a dramatic game with the spectators, seducing them into a suspension of disbelief. He uses Arkadina's seeming lack of interest in Sorin to create a false sense of security for the audience, before plunging them into an uneasy anxiety. His stage direction also implies that the actor playing Sorin mustn't indulge in any melodramatic clichés: the acting is to be as realistic as possible.

An early Method of Physical Actions

The constant interplay between big emotions and physical activities continues through Act 3 into the dialogue between mother and son surrounding the head-bandaging. Initially the task of reapplying the dressing is extremely practical and realistic, as Stanislavsky provides details of filling a glass of water, pouring it into a soup plate, mixing it with disinfectant, tearing rags, folding rags and soaking rags: the para phernalia of naturalism offsets the emotive dialogue. As passions rise, however, Stanislavsky writes various psychological gestures into the characters' demeanour, revealing how those big emotions are displaced into physical tics. Thus, we have Arkadina drumming nervously on the table and tapping her foot on the floor. These peripheral movements of her body show that, although she remains seated, she is boiling like a kettle, until the moment at which 'beside herself, she flings the end of the rolled up bandage . . . in Konstantin's face' (ibid.: 227). What Stanislavsky achieves by listing the medical details of preparing the bandage is the creation of a tragicomic resonance when he reaches Chekhov's own stage direction: *Tears the bandage off his head* (Chekhov 1990: 41). After all the attention mother pays son, Kostya rips off the dressing and hurls it at her.

In many ways, this is another early form of the Method of Physical Actions, in that Stanislavsky takes the actors from simple practical tasks through to psycho-physical gestures combining seething inner emotions with rapid physical actions. Therefore, Arkadina goes from drumming the table, to tearing the bandage to crashing her chair to the floor. The sequence, or score, of physical actions builds to a crescendo in proportion to her inner emotions. The actors' relationships with props, as well as with each other, serve as a realistic texturing of the spoken word. There is a wonderfully ironic moment at the end of the dialogue, when Trigorin arrives and Kostya runs out. To distract from her obvious distress, Arkadina starts carefully putting Trigorin's papers into his case:

her physical action stands in stark contrast to Konstantin's own destruction of his manuscripts in the final act of the play.

Playing with genre

From time to time in his production plan, Stanislavsky reveals his awareness that he was playing with dramatic forms as much as exploring new avenues of staging. Halfway through the argument between mother and son, Stanislavsky incites his actors with the words: 'To make the play more dynamic and more comprehensible to the audience, I would very much advise the actors not to be afraid of the *most glaring* realism in this scene' (cited in Balukhaty 1952: 229).

Then again, during the lovers' tiff between Arkadina and Trigorin, Stanislavsky inserts the note that she 'embraces him, kneels before him, acts a real tragedy, or rather melodrama' (ibid.: 233). He converts Arkadina's play-acting, implicit in the text, into overt vocabulary concerning theatrical forms, as she 'speaks in the tone and with the sort of pathos usually employed in melodrama' (ibid.: 235). Stanislavsky acknowledges that Arkadina has an objective to achieve – 'to seduce Trigorin' – and he encourages the actress playing the role to exploit recognisable theatrical conventions to fulfil that objective. This is a sophisticated metatheatrical device, in which the actress playing Arkadina is exploiting various dramatic forms in order that the character of Arkadina can reach her psychological objective.

The musical playout

The dialogue between Trigorin and Arkadina is the last in a series of 'duets' that comprise this highly musical act. We weave from the poignant comedy of Masha and Trigorin to the lyricism of Trigorin and Nina, followed by the high comedy of Arkadina and Sorin, which ends in an abrupt moment of potential tragedy with his fainting fit. The contrasting dialogues between Konstantin and Arkadina (tragicomedy) and Trigorin and Arkadina (comedy) bookend each other, before the orchestral finale of the act in which the entourage take leave of their estate. It is particularly worth noting in this section the way in which Stanislavsky personalises the ensemble. The character of the maid (until this point unmentioned) is shown to be wonderfully spunky, being the only one not to bow low to Arkadina, but, rather, being pictured looking displeased. Another maidservant in the crowd has a baby who starts to cry, thereby adding to the cacophony of farewell frenzy. Any sentimentality at the grand departure is entirely undercut by Polina and her plums, one small line of Chekhov's text which is turned by Stanislavsky into a whole farcical routine! It begins with Polina squeezing her way through the crowd of domestics into the front hall to give Arkadina a basket of plums. Half a page later, Arkadina goes out to the carriage, at which point Polina runs back into the dining room to fetch the plums that her mistress has (intentionally?) forgotten. Arkadina's giving of a rouble to be shared between three servants causes another crush, through which Polina once more pushes with her basket of plums, accompanied by the old retainer, Yakov, who shuffles through the crowd to retrieve a forgotten suitcase. Although Chekhov himself inserted some of the business with the plums, Stanislavsky has taken the idea to a further comical degree, from which the final moment of intimate solitude between Trigorin and Nina emerges with heightened poignancy.

From a distance of over 100 years, the way in which Stanislavsky specifies the lengths of various kisses is rather droll. Ten seconds is the duration of Nina and Trigorin's final kiss, compared with the mere five seconds granted Nina and Konstantin in Act 1. Of course we can guess the degrees of intimacy in their respective kisses, but ultimately it is the sustained moment of hiatus in the middle of the frantic departure that seems to be most important here. It is fairly unlikely that Stanislavsky stood with a stopwatch in rehearsals making sure that the kisses lasted their specified time. But the point really is that Stanislavsky's attention to detail once more illustrates his understanding of musicality, realistic acting and contradictory tempo-rhythms and atmospheres.

ACT 4

Tying up loose ends

After the vigorous departure and the sound of carriage bells at the end of the previous scene, Act 4 begins with a specified pause 'of between ten and fifteen seconds' (Stanislavsky cited in Balukhaty 1952: 247). Then Stanislavsky begins to paint with both colour and sound. The reddish glow of the stove fills the room, while the atmospheric soundscape reveals the change in season and psychological climate. Wind and rain beat against the windows causing the panes to rattle. Medvedenko enters, chilled to the marrow and stamping his feet – a stage direction which is underlined with red pencil in the prompt copy, illustrating Stanislavsky's fervour to create the feeling of an outside world, a world beyond the confines of the stage.

In this final act, Stanislavsky completes images and ideas that he has set up in the previous three acts, not least of which is the musicality of the production plan. Konstantin's piano playing becomes a literal score accompanying Polina and Masha as they make up Sorin's bed. Masha's physical actions complement the soundscape: as she 'sighs' then 'shuts the lid of the snuff box fiercely' (ibid.: 253), the contrast between the sustained sigh and the staccato snapping of the lid conjures up the contradictory emotions within Masha herself. The piano music is also used very consciously as a source of affective memory for Polina: Stanislavsky explicitly explains how Polina's thoughts in listening to the music drift back to memories of her own love affair with Dr Dorn.

Throughout the play, we have seen how Dr Dorn's inner life is manifested by his continual humming – an idea provided by Chekhov in the script and amplified by Stanislavsky in the production plan. It usually indicates that Dorn is preoccupied with something other than the present moment. This device reaches a climax in his curious exchange with Sorin, during which Stanislavsky has the able-bodied doctor almost dancing round the wheelchair-bound invalid. Over a page of dialogue between the two characters, Sorin is stuck with his dreams and his newspaper, while Dorn 'perambulates' around the room, humming. At the end of the exchange, Chekhov specifies a pause (Chekhov 1990: 53). This pause is made extremely full in Stanislavsky's production plan: Dorn is lost in his tune, Sorin is lost in his newspaper and Konstantin 'stares motionlessly in front of him. Masha looks wistfully at Konstantin, and Paulina [sic] at Dorn' (Stanislavsky cited in Balukhaly 1952: 257). Stanislavsky again uses a kind of stage close-up to take us right into the characters' very thoughts. Even when Dorn eventually sits down, it is in a rocking chair, as if he of all the characters can settle least easily.

The rocking chair is used as a very specific device during Konstantin's account of Nina's life: as the story grows sadder, Dorn's rocking becomes slower and slower, 'until at last, at the pause, he stops rocking himself altogether' (ibid.: 259). The rocking chair is seen to be an outer manifestation of Dorn's inner state. With the Method of Physical Actions, and certainly with Active Analysis, actors can strike up a relationship with anything that provides them with appropriate psychophysical information. It may be a prop, a sound, a lighting effect, or, of course, another actor! Here – for the actor playing Dorn – it is a piece of furniture.

Building tension and dissolving atmospheres

Throughout Konstantin's story of Nina, the recollections of unfortunate events in her professional or private life are given an eerie underscoring. So, when Kostya describes how Nina made 'a complete mess' of her private life, there is a pause and what Stanislavsky simply calls 'sound effects'. These are repeated when Kostya declares that her stage career 'was an even worse failure'. A pause and the same sound effects are again elicited by the debate surrounding whether she had any talent or not. (It is curious that Stanislavsky doesn't specify what the particular sound effects are.) The fourth moment occurs in response to Kostya's confession that Nina never admitted him to her hotel, and the final combination of 'pause and sound effect' reverberates after his revelation that 'She kept saying in the letters that she was a seagull' (Chekhov 1990: 54). The pay-off for the fivefold 'pause and sound effect' moments occurs when, towards the end of Konstantin's story, the pause is followed by the sound of carriage bells signalling the arrival of Arkadina. The sobering recollections of Nina are superseded by the girlish sleigh-bells of the woman who got the man.

Arkadina's arrival collides with the established atmosphere, shattering the solemnity with her kissing and chocolates and throwing of gloves. Curiously, the older woman's behaviour is seen as more girlish than the 'real' life into which Nina threw herself. The texturing of atmospheres is taken a step further by Stanislavsky's stage directions, in a way that prefigures Act 1 of *Three Sisters*, when one upstage conversation between the soldiers unwittingly comments on a downstage conversation between the three sisters. Here, in *The Seagull*, Stanislavsky stresses that Masha's sullen acknowledgement that she is married and unhappy provokes an awkward pause 'during which the conversation of the group up-stage can be heard (it is here that I would make them burst out laughing suddenly at some of Dorn's witticisms)' (Stanislavsky cited in Balukhaty 1952: 265). So, was it in fact Stanislavsky who first gave to Chekhov the idea of counterpointing stage dialogue, a technique that seemed so revolutionary and unexpected in *Three Sisters*?

Real or ridiculous? Playing with circles of attention

Stanislavsky is certainly not afraid of adding to the text on occasion. One of these moments occurs in this act when Masha sees off Medvedenko, 'giving him instructions concerning their child' (Stanislavsky cited in Balukhaty 1952: 267). Similarly, when the lotto game begins, Stanislavsky suggests that Masha call out numbers in addition to those specified by Chekhov in the script. Far from being maverick with the text, both of these suggestions enhance the realism of everyday life that Stanislavsky was keen to perpetuate. Once or twice, however, his embellishments seem a little overzealous. Chekhov writes that Konstantin starts to play a melancholy waltz off-stage, after which Arkadina steals attention by showing the company the brooch that she was recently given. Stanislavsky extends this instance to almost ridiculous ends:

> A pause. Shamrayev takes brooch and examines it in the light of the candle. The game halts for a little while. Shamrayev turns the brooch round and round before the light of the candle, while the rest look on. . . . *The Pause* [underlined in ink]: wind, rain, rattling of windows, from the distance the sound of the piano (played by Konstantin). The pause lasts ten seconds.
>
> (ibid.: 269)

Despite the excess of this stage direction, Stanislavsky is clearly trying to establish the musicality and atmosphere by means of as many different layers and textures as possible. He goes on to specify that Masha calls out the lotto numbers in a 'mournful monotonous voice' (reflecting the tone of Konstantin's piano playing), while Arkadina chats in a 'very cheerful voice' (contradicting the tone of her son's music). From time to time, Shamrayev drops his bass '*à la* Silva' impression in to make her laugh. Into this soundscape of voices and music, Stanislavsky adds Dorn's habitual humming and Sorin's timely snoring! The multiplicity of emotional reactions is heightened, not only by the words that the characters speak, but the manner in which they speak them and the accompanying noises that they make.

What Stanislavsky is doing here is creating four very distinct circles of attention. The first is within the characters' own heads, be it Masha's monotony or Dorn's humming. The second is within the room, mainly through the gregarious outbursts of Arkadina and Shamrayev during the lotto game. The third circle encompasses the rest of the house as we hear Konstantin's melancholy waltz. Every so often, Stanislavsky reminds us of the outside world: for example, 'A very long pause' as the characters exit out to dinner is followed by 'wind and rain' and interspersed with 'Animated conversation in the dining room' (ibid.: 273). The constant dynamic tension between outer world (in which Nina lives) and inner world (in which Trigorin temporarily resides) is tightened, with Konstantin psychologically trapped in a nebulous hinterland between the two.

Nina and Konstantin's final encounter

The aural textures develop when Nina arrives and, falling upon Konstantin's chest, begins to sob. We then hear 'The sound of a church-bell in the distance; in the dining room Miss Arkadina's and Shamrayev's laughter' (Stanislavsky cited in Balukhaty 1952: 275). In Act 1, Stanislavsky set up the connection between the church bell and Nina's character: now the solitude of the church bell tolling versus the sound of the dinner guests' laughing serves as a painful commentary on Nina's current situation. Curiously, Stanislavsky himself is rather coy about this device. When the laughter is heard a second time in the dining room – just at the point when Nina bursts into sobs on her line, 'And Lord help all homeless wanderers', (Chekhov 1990: 62) – he adds: 'This is a very clumsy stage effect, but it never misses with an audience. I do not, of course, insist on it' (Stanislavsky cited in Balukhaty 1952: 277). He is aware that he may be ladling on the sentiment in a potentially 'melodramatic' manner; and yet, there is a cruelty in the device which undercuts the sentiment. And – like any good producer – he doesn't want to miss a trick with the audience if it will achieve a succulent theatrical experience.

As the play draws towards its emotional climax, Stanislavsky is acutely aware of the journey on which he wants to take the audience. Whereas Chekhov writes in a pause after Kostya asks Nina why she must leave, Stanislavsky insists: 'No pause here under any circumstances' (ibid.: 279). He senses where the impetus of the scene is vital, and a pause here would only break the characters' emotional intensity. Two lines later, however, when Nina asks for a glass of water, he allows enough silence for the sound of the glass knocking against the jug to be heard, followed by a snatch of the conservation in the dining room. In other words, the tiny detail of the intimacy between Nina and Konstantin is juxtaposed with the bigger social gathering, which includes – of course – the dangerous Trigorin.

The directions provided for the last few moments of Kostya and Nina's *affaire* pile image upon image, with the howling wind and the beating rain increasing in volume as Nina recalls some of Konstantin's play. Bells toll, windows break, doors close and footsteps disappear to the sound of laughter and the knocking of the nightwatchman. The sequence concludes when 'Konstantin stands without moving, then he lets fall the glass from his hand', accompanied in the production plan by Stanislavsky's own self-deprecating comment that 'this, too, is rather a cheap stage effect!' (ibid.: 283). It is almost as if Stanislavsky can't help himself: he wants to create the maximum dramatic and emotional scene, while teetering on a knife-edge between realism and melodrama.

Drawing to a close

Chekhov knew that he was breaking all the accepted theatrical conventions with the ending of *The Seagull*, and Stanislavsky endeavoured to create a dramatic climax to a deliberately anticlimactic play. Konstantin destroys all his manuscripts (given great attention to detail by Stanislavsky, and expressed very simply by Chekhov as '*Over the next two minutes he silently tears up all his manuscripts and throws them under the desk*' (Chekhov 1990: 65)). Then the 'mob' returns. Stanislavsky creates a vast whirlwind of lively activity, with laughter and lotto, followed by a gunshot and a pause of five seconds. From the dance of action, the characters freeze in a *tableau vivant*, 'afraid to breathe' (Stanislavsky cited in Balukhaty 1952: 285), as they await the return of Dorn, who goes to discover the cause of the gunshot. Stanislavsky guides both the actors and the audience into one extreme close-up on Dorn's face: the doctor begins disconcertedly, then he 'changes the expression of his face before the eyes of the audience' (ibid.). He deflects attention from himself with his usual humming, and then 'When nobody can see him, his face again expresses concern and shock' (ibid.). Stanislavsky provides the actor with very technical facial details, which must then be justified and filled with the appropriate inner content. By these means, he keeps the spectators' attention finely focused on the doctor's face.

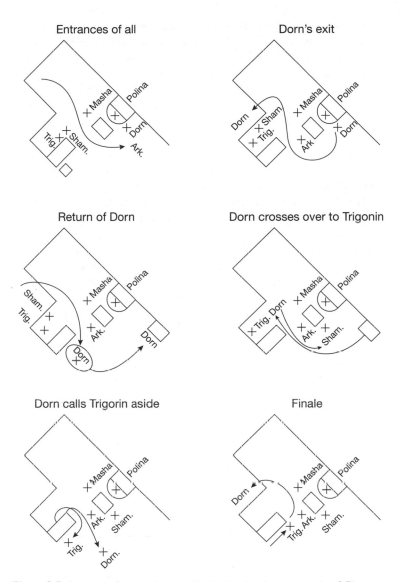

Figure 3.5 A series of ground plans illustrating the last moments of *The Seagull*, adapted from Stanislavsky's sketches (1938: 295). The scurry of activity demonstrated by this series of ground plans reveals the final moments of action in the play

Right up to the final moment, Stanislavsky is keen 'to keep the audience in suspense' (ibid.: 287). The very last stage direction in the production plan continues the musical texturing of vocal timbres (Masha's monotonous voice calls out the lotto numbers against Arkadina's soft, gay humming). At the same time, he takes the audience right to the brink of resolution, but then denies them: 'Trigorin, shaken and pale, walks over to the back of Miss Arkadina's chair where, however, he stops dead, for he cannot summon enough courage to break the terrible news to her' (ibid.). Unable to let the final line of Chekhov's text – '[Konstantin] has shot himself' (Chekhov 1990: 167) – stand alone, Stanislavsky adds these details of Trigorin's attempt to tell Arkadina. And yet he still manages to leave us hung in a moment of indecision, honouring Chekhov's desire that the audience be denied its usual theatrical expectations.

A hive of scribbled sketches fills the final page of Stanislavsky's plan, reflecting the highly choreographed sense of the entire production score (see Figure 3.5). The detail of sound, lighting, spatial relationships, physical activities, psychological gestures, intonations and pauses clearly marks *The Seagull* out as a milestone in the development of Stanislavsky's ideas. It also prefigures many of the components of his 'system'. Characters play definite actions on each other as they strive towards their own significant objectives. Naturalism, realism and symbolism brush with tragedy, comedy and absurdism in a truly inspirational production plan.

PRACTICAL EXERCISES

INTRODUCTION

The exercises in this chapter fall into three basic categories: Introduction to 'round-the-table analysis' and Stanislavsky's 'system'; Introduction to the Method of Physical Actions; and Introduction to Active Analysis. The first section is a mixture of devised exercises and some of Stanislavsky's own, while the second and third sections begin by analysing Stanislavsky's rehearsal practices to try and piece together some practical strategies.

INTRODUCTION TO 'ROUND-THE-TABLE ANALYSIS' AND STANISLAVSKY'S 'SYSTEM'

The implication of this section is that students sit round a table and analyse a text. Wrong! It's vitally important that, from the first encounter with Stanislavsky's 'system', actors understand that it's *practical* and *experiential*, not dry and intellectual. Therefore, these exercises are essentially theatre games, designed to be fun as much as informative.

RELAXATION

Muscular relaxation was the starting point for all Stanislavsky's work. So, as soon as you realise that physical relaxation liberates your imagination, the sooner you'll understand that everything is psycho-physical, even analysis of character. Stanislavsky's own exercises in 'Relaxation of Muscles' (Chapter 6 of *An Actor Prepares*) are very accessible.

Exercise 4.1

Lie on the floor, and work through the body, consciously tensing and releasing each set of muscles from the feet, the calves, the knees, the thighs, the buttocks (then the whole leg), the stomach, the chest (then the whole torso), the upper arms, the lower arms, the fists (then the whole arm), the neck, the face, the whole scalp.

Adopt a series of poses ('sitting up straight, half sitting, standing, half standing, kneeling, crouching, alone, in groups, with chairs, with a table or other furniture' (Stanislavsky 1980: 102)). As you adopt each pose, make a mental note of which muscles are involved in the task, and how few are actually needed to carry it out efficiently. Then relax whichever muscles are unnecessarily employed.

GIVEN CIRCUMSTANCES

The first component to negotiate in Stanislavsky's 'system' is 'Given Circumstances', as these determine most of the choices an actor, designer, director and even marketing manager will make about the production of a particular play. It's worth remembering that the space itself (in-the-round, street theatre, proscenium arch, black box studio) and the nature of the project (Is it a schools project or a major tour with a big television name in the leading role? Is the design 'economical' or does a large budget influence costume and set?) are just as much given circumstances as anything gleaned from the playtext and historical research. The following series of simple improvisations unlocks the importance of even the most basic facts.

Exercise 4.2: Working with ONE given circumstance

One of two volunteers selects a card on which is written a PLACE.

Having only this one piece of information, you then begin an improvised scene, using minimal furniture or props as required.

Possible places are:

- ➤ a mountain top
- ➤ grandmother's sitting room
- ➤ a hospital waiting room
- ➤ a greasy spoon café
- ➤ Brighton Beach
- ➤ the head teacher's office
- ➤ your lover's bedroom
- ➤ a lift
- ➤ a shopping mall
- ➤ a broken-down car
- ➤ the monkey house at London Zoo
- ➤ a graveyard
- ➤ the foot of the Eiffel Tower
- ➤ a railway station

Although the emphasis is on exploring one given circumstance, you also have to engage in *limitless attention to your partner* and *constant adaptation*, as all the other given circumstances (who you are, why you're here, etc.) are invented as you go along. This invention also adds the element of play, as you have to accept what the other actor says, adapt to it and build upon it to maintain a convincing and action-driven scenario.

During the first exercise, two discoveries emerge very quickly: that given circumstances are the vital building blocks out of which all plays and dialogues are constructed, and that it's incredibly difficult to work from only one specified given circumstance. So, another is introduced.

Exercise 4.3: Working with TWO given circumstances

A number of TIMES are written on cards, and two more volunteers are called up.

One of you selects a PLACE card, and one selects a TIME card. So you might find yourself in 'the boyfriend's bedroom on Christmas day' or 'the top of a mountain in spring' or 'the head teacher's office at 2 a.m.'.

Now *justification* becomes one of the components with which you have to work: after all, why on earth would you be in the head teacher's office at 2 a.m.? At the same time, you still have to pay limitless attention to each other and adapt to any other given circumstances that you each introduce into the improvisation (e.g. 'Fancy meeting you here, Grandad!', or 'Now, Biggins, what are you doing in my office at 2 a.m.?').

Possible times are:
- ➤ Sunday teatime
- ➤ the day war broke out
- ➤ 10.30 p.m. – March
- ➤ Hallowe'en
- ➤ dawn
- ➤ 2.00 a.m. – May
- ➤ New Year's Day 2000
- ➤ lunchtime
- ➤ yesterday afternoon
- ➤ ten to midnight on Christmas Eve
- ➤ August Bank Holiday

OBJECTIVES

Even with the addition of a second given circumstance, actors often find the dramatic action hard to maintain. It quickly transpires that the difficulty is that they don't know *why* they're there, or to put it more succinctly – they haven't got an objective. So the next stage is to introduce *objectives*.

Exercise 4.4

Two volunteers select a PLACE and a TIME card.

Then you're each given a card on which is written an objective. While both of you know the two given circumstances, you're only aware of your own objective. Often, the more opposing the objectives, the greater will be the dramatic tension, but – more importantly – the harder you'll have to work to attain your own objective.

Possible objectives could be:
- ➤ 1a to make yourself understood
- ➤ 1b to get your partner to leave the room

- ➤ 2a to disguise your true identity
- ➤ 2b to find out the truth

- 3a   to create a party atmosphere
- 3b   to arouse suspicion
- 4a   to discover the enemy
- 4b   to lull into a false sense of security
- 5a   to win admirers
- 5b   to deflect attention
- 6a   to control the situation
- 6b   to control the situation
- 7a   to find out who the other person is while concealing who you are
- 7b   to find out who the other person is while concealing who you are

Note that 6 and 7 involve the same objectives: this can also produce some very intriguing results. You don't have to be too obvious with your objective. It's far more interesting to be inventive and indirect: after all, it's not a competition, it's the creation of dramatic tension.

Afterwards, the rest of the group can hazard a guess at each volunteer's objective.

INNER ACTIONS

The tendency with these exercises may be that the spoken word dominates the improvisation. So the next ingredient to add is *inner action*.

Exercise 4.5

Again, two volunteers select a PLACE and a TIME card.

Then, you're each given a card on which is written a line of dialogue. This can be from anything – from Chekhov to *Friends*.

For the duration of the improvisation, you can say nothing but the words on the card. These words may be spoken once, or repeated in full or in part, as often as you deem appropriate.

The major rule, however, is that no words other than those that appear on the card can be spoken at any point. This means that your task is to find the precise moment when your line of text fits absolutely with your own inner action and with the silent action existing between yourself and the other actor. So you have to listen to the spatial dynamics between you both as much as to the words that you speak.

Possible lines of dialogue (from Chekhov's *The Seagull*):

- ➤ 'You're so lovely . . .'
- ➤ 'I'm not going to set foot inside this place again.'
- ➤ 'How boring these people are.'
- ➤ 'What's the matter with you?'
- ➤ 'I'm too simple to understand you.'
- ➤ 'Maybe this is the very thing I needed.'
- ➤ 'I'm not ashamed of my love for you.'
- ➤ 'I'm sorry.'
- ➤ 'I had a feeling we'd see each other again.'
- ➤ 'Shut the window, there's a draught'.

Possible lines from contemporary plays:

- ➤ 'Touch me and I'll scream.'
- ➤ 'Don't give me none of that cheek either.'
- ➤ 'You have such beautiful hands.'
- ➤ 'I'm not meeting anyone.'
- ➤ 'I want you to come with me before he gets back.'
- ➤ 'You going anywhere?'
- ➤ 'Is your lover coming today?'
- ➤ 'I'm not perfect, I know.'
- ➤ 'I knew it wasn't right.'
- ➤ 'I thought I was a bird.'
- ➤ 'Tell me what you want me to do.'

NB: The aim is not to say your own line as early as possible and then think, 'Phew! I've done my bit. Now how's the other actor going to get her line out?' The task is to work together collaboratively and attentively, with – of course – a healthy whack of play. It's important to stress that the improvisation doesn't finish as soon as the second person has said her line. It may well be that, in the silence following the second line of text, a whole new dynamic unfolds, allowing the improvisation to continue (albeit silently) for some moments beyond the spoken word.

For all its apparent simplicity (two given circumstances and one line of text each), it's an incredibly complex improvisation, demanding great complicity between the two actors. It also unlocks *subtext* and the action inherent within *pauses*, as each actor waits to find the moment when their line of text is appropriate.

ACTIONS

Exercise 4.6

To make the previous exercise even more complex but precise, the volunteers each select an 'action' from another set of cards. This action dictates the way in which you have to say your line once you've found the moment when it's appropriate to speak it. The action chosen inevitably gives more information about the relationship between the two characters, and so provides you with a subtext underlying that one line of text. It's tricky, but it's fun!

Possible actions to be played on each line:

- ➤ to shock
- ➤ to frighten
- ➤ to bewitch
- ➤ to reassure
- ➤ to amuse
- ➤ to provoke
- ➤ to impress
- ➤ to intrigue
- ➤ to persuade
- ➤ to charm
- ➤ to belittle
- ➤ to confuse
- ➤ to infuriate
- ➤ to soothe
- ➤ to uplift

SENSE MEMORY AND EMOTION MEMORY

Much of Stanislavsky's 'system' simply reminds us that we already possess the tools that an actor needs (body, imagination, emotions and human experiences). It's just a matter of reawakening and provoking those tools so that they're available to us at any chosen moment.

It's the same with emotion memory, an element of Stanislavsky's 'system' which can seem rather daunting. And yet it's nothing more than a part of the matrix of human responses by which we live our daily lives. The following exercise, therefore, is extremely simple (though it does require some preparation on the part of the workshop leader). Through its simplicity, it can access a wide range of emotional responses with the minimum amount of psychological effort. (In many ways, it can seem like a party game, and yet the emotional information that it releases must be taken seriously and treated with integrity.)

The exercise involves stimulating each of the five senses separately and allowing participants to share with each other the images and experiences that are conjured up.

Exercise 4.7: Sensory stimulations

All the participants are blindfolded (or eyes are kept closed) in a circle while they *feel* a number of objects, one at a time. These might include a wire scouring pad, a teddy bear, a sponge, a rubber ball, a metal box, a feather boa, a plastic duck, a wedge of polystyrene, or a blob of plasticine: in other words, objects with varying textures, temperatures, shapes and emotional connotations.

Without identifying the objects, the participants are asked to share their immediate responses.

A variation of this exercise is to give everyone a glove – woollen, leather, velvet, lace, mitten, long, fingerless, etc. – and to invite more imaginative suggestions as to what colour it might be, who might wear it, is it old or new, female or male, etc. The only stimulus is the physical touch, paying careful attention to the information (actual or imaginative) that the recipient takes from the glove's feel.

While the participants remain blindfolded, a number of plastic cartons are passed around containing various *smelly* substances. These could include lavender, stale beer, strawberry bubble bath, fresh soil, marmite, washing-up liquid, coffee, cigarette butts, or chocolate. Again, the participants share their instant reactions, whether those responses be images, memories or emotions, but without giving away the identity of the smells. It's the stimulation of the senses that's important, not the identification of the stimulants.

A number of items are placed on cocktail sticks in front of the participants who simultaneously pick up and *taste* the same object, and share their responses. Suggested foods are a chunk of bread, a salted chipstick, a marshmallow, a little pickled onion and an orange-flavoured sweet. (Curiously, taste seems to arouse some of the most potent memories: the chipstick in particular frequently conjures up very specific childhood experiences.)

Remaining blindfolded, the participants *listen* to a selection of music and, in response to what they hear, they're encouraged to move about the room in any way they want to. Now the sense memory exercise merges with a psycho-physical experience, as the emotions conjured up by the music are converted into physical expression and spatial dynamics. Of course any music or soundscape can be used, as long as the rhythms, atmospheres and tempi contrast with each other: for example, African drumming, Irish harp, Turkish wind instruments, Russian gypsy songs, and particularly emotive music from films such as *Conquest of Paradise* (Vangelis) or *Gladiator* (Zimmer and Gerrard).

The final stimulation to the senses is *sight*. The most straightforward way to activate sight memory is to ask the participants to picture themselves and all the other people in the room, and to remember (or imagine) the details of their faces and the clothes that they're wearing.

Then, when they're ready, they take off their blindfolds and look – as if for the first time – at their colleagues, to understand how much (or how little) information their imaginations have absorbed. Thereafter, the workshop leader can show them a series of pictures: suggestions include a newborn baby, a cartoon character, a victim of torture, an Escher-type picture, where the eye plays games with the image, a beautiful landscape and a naked body. Alternatively, participants may be asked to bring to the session their own evocative pictorial images and exchange them with the rest of the group.

The simplicity of this series of exercises reminds students how extensive their own inner encyclopaedia of emotional references may be. It also demonstrates how many of those emotional references can be evoked with very little psychological contortion. There are more oblique allusions to emotion memory in the exercises below. However, it's important for young actors to understand the way in which the psycho-physical aspects of their craft can be accessed through very direct, almost childlike, inroads.

By the end of this Introduction, students will be acquainted with the fundamental components of the 'system'. They will have experienced given circumstances, objectives, actions, justification, adaptation, a sense of play and emotion memory, without having sat down once at a table with a piece of text. The main element that has still to be tackled in terms of 'round-the-table analysis' is the division of text into *bits* or 'units' of action. To avoid this process becoming dry and intellectual, it's worth leaving it until more of the fun, practical elements have been absorbed. Then, when the group is ready, simply sit round with a piece of text and read it, stopping and noting where the subject of the play evolves, or a character enters or exits, or where a particular character's tactic clearly changes. Label the 'bit' of action, and find appropriate names for the characters' objectives. As discussed in Chapter 2, the label for a 'bit' can be fairly dispassionate (e.g. 'The Interrogation'), though the objectives should be expressed through verbs (e.g. 'I want to get him to leave me alone'; 'I want to force her to confess'). These titles needn't be set in stone, as the chances are that, once the actors get up on their feet and start rehearsing, the objectives will be tweaked and fine-tuned. (See Figure 4.1 for an example of textual analysis.)

INTRODUCTION TO THE METHOD OF PHYSICAL ACTIONS

Unpacking the components of the Method of Physical Actions is rather tricky, as it's a rehearsal method, and – as with all rehearsal methods – its success or otherwise is hugely dependent on the director's imagination! The most useful sources for discovering the way in which it worked are *Stanislavski Directs* (Gorchakov 1994) and *Stanislavski on Opera* (Stanislavsky and Rumyantsev 1998). Both of these books were written by actors working with Stanislavsky at the time of his final experiments. As such, they are treasure troves full of wildly imaginative ideas that he invented for particular scenes in a diversity of plays and operas. His own *Creating a Role* (Stanislavsky 2000b) is also hugely valuable, as it covers a fifteen-year span and reveals how the various components of the rehearsal system emerged.

Taking these texts as a starting point, this section will dissect the Method of Physical Actions, and then supply some simple games and exercises, which can be used to supplement rehearsals on any particular play. Basically, however, teachers and workshop leaders are rather left to their own devices in terms of the scripts that they choose and the imaginative stimulations that they provide for their students and actors. That said, a combination of the books mentioned above and the exercises suggested here should equip an intrepid experimenter with sufficient examples to risk having a go! Let's start by looking briefly at Stanislavsky's own ideas about the Method of Physical Actions to piece together why and how it can be put into action.

COMPONENTS WITHIN THE METHOD OF PHYSICAL ACTIONS

As we saw in Chapter 2, the essential ingredient in the Method of Physical Actions is a 'score of physical actions'. We also saw that two words appear repeatedly: 'logic' and 'coherence'. These are the defining nouns in compiling that score of actions. So, the challenge in rehearsals is to break down every moment of a play into a series of actions, each of which logically depends upon the next. It took Stanislavsky some years to formulate a precise rehearsal technique, but if we look at two of the major stages in his fifteen-year development (as detailed in *Creating a Role*), we can start to piece together some useful rehearsal strategies.

WOE FROM WIT (1916–20): AN EARLY SEQUENCE OF EXERCISES TO SUPPLEMENT THE METHOD OF PHYSICAL ACTIONS

In this – the first stage of his developing Method of Physical Actions – Stanislavsky divides the actor's work on a role into three 'periods': (1) The Period of Study; (2) The Period of Emotional Experience; and (3) The Period of Physical Embodiment. In each of these sections, there are exercises and strategies that might help us as experimenters to understand the psycho-physical layers within the Method of Physical Actions.

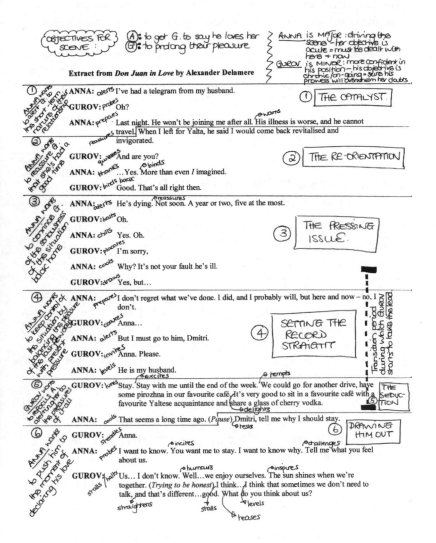

Figure 4.1 (a and b) Units and objectives on an extract from Alexander Delamere's *Don Juan in Love* (2001)

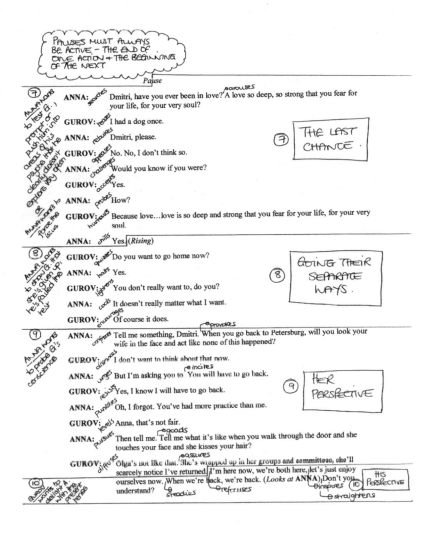

PAUSES MUST ALWAYS BE ACTIVE - THE END OF ONE ACTION + THE BEGINNING OF THE NEXT

Pause

ANNA: (*searches*) Dmitri, have you ever been in love? [arouses] A love so deep, so strong that you fear for your life, for your very soul?

GUROV: (*teases*) I had a dog once.

ANNA: (*rebukes*) Dmitri, please.

GUROV: (*eases*) No. No, I don't think so.

ANNA: (*challenges*) Would you know if you were?

GUROV: (*accepts*) Yes.

ANNA: (*probes*) How?

GUROV: (*humours*) Because love...love is so deep and strong that you fear for your life, for your very soul.

ANNA: (*chills*) Yes. (*Rising*)

⑦ THE LAST CHANCE

GUROV: (*quizzes*) Do you want to go home now?

ANNA: (*halts*) Yes.

GUROV: (*ignores*) You don't really want to, do you?

ANNA: (*cool*) It doesn't really matter what I want.

GUROV: (*encourages*) Of course it does.

⑧ GOING THEIR SEPARATE WAYS

ANNA: (*confronts*) [provokes] Tell me something, Dmitri. When you go back to Petersburg, will you look your wife in the face and act like none of this happened?

GUROV: (*dismisses*) I don't want to think about that now.

ANNA: (*urges*) [re-incites] But I'm asking you to. You will have to go back.

GUROV: (*resists*) Yes, I know I will have to go back.

ANNA: (*punishes*) Oh, I forgot. You've had more practice than me.

GUROV: (*levels*) Anna, that's not fair.

ANNA: (*pursues*) [goads] Then tell me. Tell me what it's like when you walk through the door and she touches your face and she kisses your hair?

GUROV: (*diffuses*) [reassures] Olga's not like that. She's wrapped up in her groups and committees, she'll scarcely notice I've returned. I'm here now, we're both here, let's just enjoy ourselves now. When we're back, we're back. (*Looks at ANNA*) [inspires] Don't you understand? [steadies] [refuses] [straightens]

⑨ HER PERSPECTIVE

⑩ HIS PERSPECTIVE

Figure 4.1 (*continued*)

Stage 1: The Period of Study

The first thing to do, of course, is:

- **Read the play**

Most of us underestimate the impact of our first encounter with a text. And yet it can be one of the most fruitful parts of the rehearsal process. So, it's vitally important that the right conditions are created before embarking on the reading – not at the bus stop, not in a café, but somewhere where you won't be disturbed. In this way, you can allow yourself to be most open to the 'unexpected and direct' impressions, 'the unpremeditated', the 'unprejudiced' 'embryo of the image to be formed' (Stanislavsky 2000b: 3). Whatever arouses you in this first reading should be deliciously savoured, as this first enthusiastic urge can fuel major creative decisions in the way you develop your role.

- **Ask questions**

It's important to remember that, although the Method of Physical Actions is a practical approach to rehearsal, it relies on a detailed understanding of the text, not so very different from the round-the-table work. The purpose of textual analysis is not only to study the playwright's work, it's also for you, the actor, to search out the vibrant material in yourself (through your five senses, your emotional memories and your intellectual responses). This kind of provocative analysis consists of endless questioning, and Stanislavsky specifies seven planes of questions that you should ask about the play:

1   *External plane*: What are the plot, events and facts, and what form do they take? (This phase basically involves structural analysis of what the playwright has written.)
2   *Plane of social situation*: What class and nationality do the characters belong to? What is the historical setting? (Again this is factual information, but the answers start to conjure up certain psychological and behavioural choices that characters may make.)
3   *Literary plane*: What are the ideas in the text? What is the style of the writing?
4   *Aesthetic plane*: What are the details of the theatrical and artistic production? How do the contents of the play dictate the choices made by the set designer?

5   *Psychological plane*: What's going on beneath the text – the inner action? What are the characters' feelings? How, in fact, are the roles characterised?
6   *Physical plane*: What are the external characteristics of the dramatis personae? What are their objectives and actions?
7   *Plane of personal creative feelings*: How do you feel about the play? (This plane is dependent on everything that the individual actors bring to the production, including the answers to the previous six questions.) (List adapted from Stanislavsky 2000b: 11.)

These layers of analytical work take us deeper and deeper into the text: Stanislavsky describes the process as going from the 'periphery' (the words on a page) to the 'centre' (the actors' inner creative state).

- **Get your imagination going**

Having asked all the analytical questions, it's time to start personalising the answers. So close your eyes and put yourself imaginatively into the surroundings of the play. Picture the house or environment in which it is set. Picture yourself walking up the path to the house, climbing the steps, knocking on the door, turning the knob, finding the door open, entering the cool hall, walking noisily over the marble tiles towards an opulent staircase, and so on.

With any imaginary exercise, Stanislavsky stresses the importance of a logical sequence of actions. You mustn't miss out a single step, or your imagination won't believe in what you're doing and your whole sense of faith in the scenario will collapse. Stanislavsky suggests that it's a good idea to imagine the props and furniture as well: feel the cold of the door handle, heave the heavy oak door open, trip up on the rug. If you can connect with an imaginary object in this way, at the same time as developing a score of actions, you can provoke your emotion memory and increase your personal sense of 'I am' in the role.

- **Appraise the facts**

'Appraising the facts' means focusing on the actual events in the play. Imagine encountering the other characters. Struggle with their objectives, see who wins and how you have to adapt your own tactics to achieve your task. If you can commit to this imaginary challenge, you may discover where your own psychology merges with that of the character, all with very little strain. As Stanislavsky puts it:

> To appraise the facts is to take all the alien life created by the playwright and make it [your] own. To appraise the facts is to find the key to the riddle of the inner life of a character which lies hidden under the text of the play.
>
> (Stanislavsky 2000b: 42)

For Stanislavsky, the work doesn't stop there. So:

- **Repeat the above**

Each time you repeat the imaginative exercises, there'll be tiny changes, to which you have to adapt. Here you'll find the novelty, the unexpectedness and the joy of constantly refreshing and stimulating your own sense of 'I am' in the role.

Stage 2: The Period of Emotional Experience

- **Compile an imaginary 'score of actions'**

So far, all the work in Stanislavsky's 'Period of Study' has been independent and private, using imagination to prepare the actor for the creative journey from self to character. The next phase begins that creative journey towards the emotional experience of the part. At this point, Stanislavsky shows us very clearly how to compile a score of actions. Taking a scene from *Woe from Wit*, he begins by working from his own personality:

> I have just returned from abroad; without going home I have driven up in a heavy travelling coach, drawn by four horses, to the gates of the house which is almost another home to me. Now my coach has stopped and the coachman has called the yardman to open the gates to the courtyard. What do I desire in this moment?
>
> (Stanislavsky 2000b: 56–7)

The answer to the question 'What do I desire?' gives him his psychological objective. So: *I desire to hasten the moment of my meeting with Sophia my lover, something I have dreamed of for so long*. He then adds a whole series of physical obstacles, such as waiting for the tardy yardman, and psychological obstacles, such as having to be polite to the old folks who greet him. These physical (outer) and psychological (inner) obstacles provoke a series of actions, albeit imaginary at this point, which he has to undertake if he is to achieve his objective. So:

1   *I must speak to the yardman, be agreeable, exchange greetings.*
2   *I must quickly rouse the sleepy doorman.*
3   *I desire to greet the dog, and pet this old friend of mine.*
4   *I must now say how do you do to the doorman, be nice to him, exchange greetings.*
5   *I must greet the steward and the housekeeper too, I must ask about Sophia. Where is she? Is she well? Is she up?*

What do I desire at this moment?

6   *I want to get to my main goal quickly, see Sophia . . .*

(adapted from Stanislavsky 2000b: 71–3)

This example shows exactly what Stanislavsky means by creating a score of actions (though – I repeat – it's still imaginary at this point). We have a major objective, carried out by means of smaller objectives, and interspersed with purely physical actions ('getting out of the carriage, ringing the doorbell, running up the stairs, and so forth' (ibid.: 58)). There is a logic and a coherence.

To summarise the two stages so far, 'The Period of Study' is a process of analysing the script imaginatively to arouse the actor's 'creative desire' to play the role. 'The Period of Emotional Experience' is still imaginative, independent work, but through it the actor can begin to experience an emotional urgency to spring into 'creative action'.

Stage 3: The Period of Physical Embodiment

•   Lure your body into action

Having approached the play imaginatively, it's now time to get physical. Stanislavsky again stresses how important it is to start with the sense of 'I am'. Therefore, whatever play you're working on, you need to pose two questions – one objective, one subjective – which will merge your self with your character. Taking the *Woe from Wit* example, Stanislavsky's *objective* question for the character is: 'What do men in love do when, after an absence of years, they are driving to see the lady of their dreams?' (Stanislavsky 2000b: 88). The *subjective* question for himself as he sits in a taxi going to the theatre is: 'What would I do if I, as now, were driving in a cab . . . not going to the theatre, [but] going to see *her* . . . ?' In other words, you take real-life situations that are 'Here, Today, Now' and you connect them with the play to lure your body into the fictional circumstances.

These three stages of preparation, Period of Study, Period of Emotional Experience and Period of Physical Embodiment can be applied to any text. It's simply a question of the director or workshop leader proposing suitable situations for the participants to imagine. 'Study' can clearly be done collectively. 'Emotional Experience' is inherently independent work, though directors could loosely guide actors through appropriate scenarios. 'Physical Embodiment' begins independently but quickly develops into improvisations with other actors. These improvisations should always begin with 'Here, Today, Now' to develop a sense of connection, or 'I am', between the actor and the scene. This should prevent early characterisations from becoming clichéd and formal.

OTHELLO (1930–3): A LATER SEQUENCE OF EXERCISES TO SUPPLEMENT THE METHOD OF PHYSICAL ACTIONS

The more we read about the way in which Stanislavsky worked, the more we understand that many of his examples stem from his inventive imagination rather than from any formal processes that can be turned into a blueprint. This should be seen as a liberation for anyone attempting the Method of Physical Actions and not an inhibition. Analyse a text, construct a score of physical actions, repeat that score to test and fine-tune its logic and coherence, and gradually introduce text. Within this sequence, anything goes!

That said, there are a number of new ideas which arise with *Othello* (the second phase of the Method's development) which clarify the process. What is interesting here is that the order in which elements of rehearsal are approached changes significantly from the work on *Woe from Wit*. The stages now are: First Acquaintance; Creating the Physical Life of the Role; and Analysis, before finishing up with Checking the Work Done and Summing Up.

Stage 1: First Acquaintance

Once again, Stanislavsky reiterates the significance of an actor's first reading of a play.

Stage 2: Creating the Physical Life of the Role

Now the process heads straight for physical action. Gone are the extensive personal investigations of imaginary actions: immediately, the actors and director begin to uncover the score of physical actions. The example that Stanislavsky uses to illustrate how this is done is the opening scene between Roderigo and Iago:

1   They enter and make sure no one is around.
2   They check the palace windows.
3   They throw stones at the windows to wake the household.
4   As that isn't working, they start making more noise to stir the house.

These actions are so simple and yet, if they're carried out with total conviction, the actors' sense of faith in those actions should evoke real feelings. As with *Woe from Wit*, the actors repeat the sequence of physical actions, checking each moment to see where the logic is missing and whether they believe in what they're doing.

Stage 3: Analysis

It's only after these first attempts to put the play on its feet that analysis is brought in. As with *Woe from Wit*, the emphasis of the analysis is on compiling various facts, including the Six Big Questions: Who? When? Where? Why? For what reason? How? Compiling the facts leads to a three stage assimilation of the information:

1   Listing the facts.
2   Appraising the facts; this involves personalising the facts of the play by asking the question:

> What circumstances of my own inner life – which of my personal human ideas, desires, efforts, qualities, inborn gifts and shortcomings – can oblige me as a man and as an actor to have an attitude toward people and events such as those of the character I am portraying?
>
> (Stanislavsky 2000b: 181)

3   Justifying the facts.

The analysis is never purely intellectual. All the time, imagination, a sense of 'I am' and emotional memory are drafted into the process, so that the actors find themselves penetrating deeper and deeper into the text, on one hand, and into their own creative resources, on the other hand.

Stage 4: Checking the Work Done and Summing Up

Stanislavsky's summary of the rehearsal method for *Othello* is extremely useful:

1　Put the scripts down and recall anything you can about the play from your memory. What you don't remember is as useful as what you do remember.
2　Draw out your intuitive responses, remembering that your first acquaintance with a script is often the most fruitful.
3　Reread the whole play to refresh your memory.
4　As a company, write down an account of the events in the play (paying attention to the facts of the play and the physical actions of the character).
5　Improvise the first scene in response to the facts that you've recorded and in terms of the physical actions that you've discovered.
6　Keep repeating these improvisations, sharpening the sequence of physical actions. Gradually, the physical actions provided by the playwright and suggested by the director will be transmuted into your own.
7　Introduce words into the improvisations. At first, these words should be your own, so that you can carry your objective powerfully forward. Little by little, the director will prompt you with words from the script. In this way, the transition from your own words to those of the character becomes painless and surreptitious.
8　Reread the play to absorb more information and more of the text.
9　Learn the script. This will be easy, as you find that what initially seemed like the author's alien actions have now become wholly your own.

SUGGESTED EXERCISES

Stanislavsky's details of *Woe from Wit* and *Othello* are incredibly useful in terms of their underlying philosophy, but of course they're very specific to the particular plays. Here are some suggested exercises by means of which you can get inside some of the underlying principles of the Method of Physical Actions.

A technical approach to consecutive actions

- **Isolated acts**

This very technical exercise is hidden in *An Actor Prepares* (Chapter 6, 'Relaxation of Muscles') and yet it's a simple but effective way of illustrating how physicality and psychology interact.

Exercise 4.8

Stand with both arms folded in front of you like a Native American, with the right arm lying on top of the left.

First, the elbow is lifted then lowered, then the wrist, then the knuckles, then the fingers. This creates a wave movement along the limb. (See Figure 4.2.)

If you start at the elbow (with the impulse coming from the shoulder), this is a central to peripheral movement; if you start at the fingertips and move to the elbow, this is peripheral to central. The significance of this physical differentiation is in fact psychological. A person who always begins with the periphery (moving to the centre) is searching, asking questions of the universe. The person who creates movements from the centre to the periphery is giving answers to the world and making bold statements. This idea is continued below.

- **Consecutive acts**

Exercise 4.9

The important way in which isolated acts combine to form a sequence of consecutive acts is revealed by simply walking forwards and backwards.

Walk forwards, noticing how the movement begins at your hips, then moves to your knees, your ankles and your heels, and finishes with the

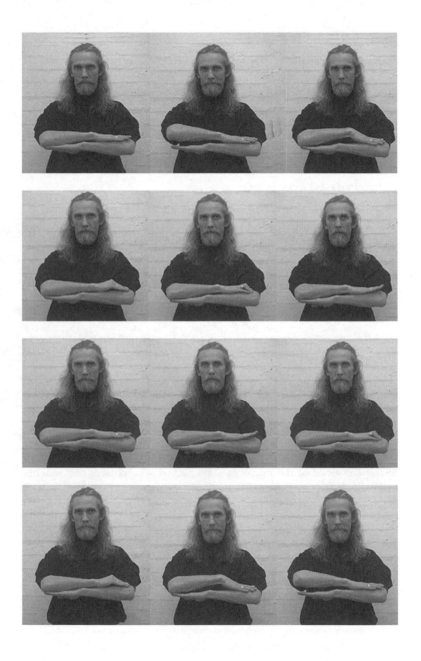

energy passing from your toes to the ground. You can see where you're going, you know what you want, and you go there and get it. You have no questions.

Now walk backwards. Notice how you begin with your toes, taking information from the floor. Feel the different inner sensation when you can't see where you're going. You're full of questions. Where is the floor? Is it solid tarmac or thin ice? Is it a wide road or a narrow ledge?

As you take that information from the ground through your toes, feel the movement proceed from the periphery up through your heels, ankles, knees and hips to the centre.

Exercise 4.10

Another simple exercise is to imagine putting your hand into a bath of water. First of all, imagine that you don't know the water's temperature: the fingertips (the periphery) go first, asking the question: 'Is is hot or cold?' Then the information passes from finger to hand to elbow to arm to body.

Imagine you've dropped a precious gold ring into a pond. The objective is strong: you want to retrieve the ring. You aren't interested in asking questions about the temperature of the water, you are interested in pursuing your (centrally, viscerally activated) objective.

Notice how your psycho-physical action moves from the centre via shoulder to elbow to wrist to knuckle and to fingers as you grasp the imaginary ring before it disappears into the silt.

Creating a dialogue: score of inner actions

Exercise 4.11

Eight participants are each asked to give one line of dialogue of any nature, so that a script of eight lines is produced.

Figure 4.2 (facing) Isolated acts: wave movement along the arm, demonstrated by Russian director, Vladimir Ananyev. The isolation of joints in the arm articulates a wave motion, as described in *An Actor Prepares* (Stanislavsky 1980: 108)

Working in pairs, compile a scene, using only these sentences. You can't change the words, but you can alter the order in which the sentences are spoken. This task requires you to compile a score of inner as well as physical actions that has an absolute logic and out of which the words arise naturally.

Keep repeating your score of inner/outer actions until your sense of faith in what you're doing is consolidated.

An example of a random series of sentences might be:

- ➤ 'Why did you do that?'
- ➤ 'That would be fantastic.'
- ➤ 'He didn't really, did he?'
- ➤ 'Two, no milk.'
- ➤ 'It's definitely finished.'
- ➤ 'I can't remember if I did or not.'
- ➤ 'What did she mean?'
- ➤ 'The Mayor of Dudley, probably.'

Creating an inner dialogue: working with an object

However odd this next exercise may sound when you read it, give it a go and surprise yourself! (A full account of it can be found in Merlin (2001: 59–61). Russian director, Vladimir Ananyev, first introduced me to it.)

Exercise 4.12

Place a garment on the floor in front of you.

Imagine that this object is extremely valuable or important (although you don't need to know at the outset why it is so significant).

For the duration of the exercise, you can move close to the object or far away from it, always allowing it to affect you in whatever way your imagination provokes. But you must never touch it! However important it may be, your underlying objective is 'to prevent yourself from touching the object':

> This objective instantly establishes an inner contradiction: if you have to prevent yourself from doing something, it suggests that part of you wants to do it, and part of you certainly doesn't. There's a dynamic set up between attraction and repulsion, between desire and denial.
>
> (Merlin 2001: 60)

Most participants find that, although they have no idea what's going to happen when they begin the exercise, very quickly a host of imaginative impulses come into their heads. One minute they love the object, then they resent its power over them, then they want to hit it, stamp on it, then protect it, then examine it, explore it, reject it. The simplicity of the exercise stimulates a myriad of contradictory reactions and interconnections between the actor and the object, while all the time there's an unbroken line between inner (psychological) and outer (physical) actions.

The letter

This exercise again explores work with an object and a score of physical actions, yet it also throws up other components from Stanislavsky's 'system' relating to the Method of Physical Actions.

Exercise 4.13

A room is laid out very simply with one chair, one table and a sofa. Somewhere in the room is an unopened letter. (These are actual letters to be prepared beforehand by the workshop leader.)

Possible letters to be used:

➤ A letter from the bank manager saying that an overdraft has been run up without prior negotiation, so now all cheques and cash withdrawals will incur a £28 charge.

➤ A note from a secret admirer who has been watching the reader of the letter and would like to meet.

➤ A chain letter with the usual veiled threats if the chain is broken.

➤ A fond letter from a friend or parent.

➤ Notification that you're the lucky winner of £2,000 on telephone confirmation of your name and address.

Enter the room as if it were your bedroom (at college, at home, or in a hotel).

At some point, you notice the letter and pick it up to read it.

You must *actually* read the letter, allowing the contents to affect your inner state of being.

Then, when you're ready, leave the room.

It's as simple as that! And yet the exercise is full of all sorts of hidden factors:

1 *Given circumstances*: What do you 'bring' into the scene with you, in terms of where have you been? Are you happy to be back in your room? Are you in a hurry? Is it late at night coming home from a club? Is it mid-afternoon having returned from a boring meeting?

2 *Solitude in public*: The whole activity is carried out as if no one were watching: you don't have to 'telegraph' anything to the audience. 'Cut ninety per cent!' was one of Stanislavsky's favourite mottos, and this exercise is great for reassuring actors of how little they need to 'add' in order for the audience to understand what's going on.

3 *Emotion memory*: You need to remember your relationship to that room, as well as feeling the inner affect that the contents of the letter have on you.

4 *Tempo-rhythm*: The contents of the letter will inevitably change your tempo-rhythm according to whether it's good news or bad, and according to whether you came into the room with a buoyant or deflated energy. Therefore, the way you exit the room will carry with it different psycho-physical information from that which you brought into the scene. In other words, the journey of the improvisation will clearly have a beginning, a middle and an end.

5 *Moment of orientation*: This will be discussed further in the exercises on Active Analysis, but suffice it to say that, when you arrive in the room, you must allow for a **moment of orientation**. If there's an unopened letter, it may well be that someone broke in, or maybe the door has been left open when you know full well that you'd locked it.

6 *Working with a prop*: The important thing about this exercise is that nothing must be mimed. Miming props disconnects your emotion memory, as all your attention goes to your skill at miming the props, rather than listening to your 'inner' process. Also, the challenge of this exercise is to see how far the given props (table, chair, sofa) can be used to convey objectives. So, for example, if you decide that you've returned to the room hurriedly to await the arrival of your boyfriend, the constant adjusting of the table to the exact position, or practising sitting in the chair at the most

flattering angle, can convey your excited anxiety as much as any tidying away of imaginary props might do.

7   *Moment of decision*: This is vital. The technical aspect of the scene is about having a dialogue with a prop and how that affects the score of physical actions. So it's important that the appropriate moment of decision is taken as to when you pick up the letter. Is it seen immediately? If so, is it opened immediately? Is it hidden under the sofa? Were you expecting this letter? Had you lost it and now you've suddenly found it? The moment of decision is the turning point in the scene. It incites the next piece of action (i.e. the reading of the letter), which in turn takes the scene in a whole new direction.

8   All these elements inform the main purpose of the exercise, which is to explore the unbroken line of simple physical actions in order to attain a larger psychologically driven objective.

Once again, this is a very simple exercise, and each participant's version will be different. Yet it's packed with many issues for exploration and discussion, and it can supplement the rehearsal of a specific text (which is essentially what the Method of Physical Actions is for).

INTRODUCTION TO ACTIVE ANALYSIS

As we saw in Chapter 1, Active Analysis is very similar to the Method of Physical Actions, the subtle difference being that it allows for more chaotic, illogical results. What this really means is that the psycho-physical aspect of the work often ignites the *emotion's* logic (or illogic) before it triggers the *brain's* ability to construct a score of physical actions. As with the Method of Physical Actions, Active Analysis is a rehearsal approach. Although it's grounded in psycho-physical actor-training, it's not the actor-training itself. This renders it difficult to break down into simple exercises, and, once again, the onus is on the director to be sparky and imaginative. As actor, Vasily Toporkov, described it: 'This unusual method requires of the director vigilance, persistence, the ability to interest the actors and awaken their imagination' (1998: 165). In fact, Toporkov's account of *Dead Souls* and *Tartuffe* (see Toporkov 1998), along with Stanislavsky's own notes on *The Inspector General* (see Stanislavsky 2000b), are terrifically useful. What emerges is that Active Analysis is not only a rehearsal format, it's a philosophy about acting. So, the following ('philosophical') points should be allied to the step-by-step practical account detailed (from Sharon Carnicke) in Chapter 1 (see pp. 34–5).

DEAD SOULS (1932)

• Connect with your own psychology

One of the key purposes behind Active Analysis is for the actors to connect themselves (totally, but artistically) with their characters' journey. This means that the director's job is principally concerned with asking questions, rather than giving directions. He or she has the exciting, though difficult, challenge of reconnecting the actors with their own psychologies, of finding a trigger that means something to them and of asking the right questions. In Toporkov's account of *Dead Souls*, the main words that keep appearing are 'simple', 'clear' and 'true'. All the questions that Stanislavsky asked his actors 'astounded us with their simplicity, lucidity, concreteness' (Toporkov 1998: 81). Therefore, a director has to keep a clear focus on what the actors are presenting in improvisations, and use a laser-sharp insight to guide them carefully towards both what they as actors have in their personal, psychological repertoires and what the playwright's characters need.

• Connect with your partner's psychology

One of the main differences between the Method of Physical Actions and Active Analysis as it emerges in Toporkov's account of *Dead Souls* is that the line of physical actions (and the sense of truth in those physical actions) depends wholly upon your on-stage partner. The 'moment of orientation' is, therefore, vital, as the look in your partner's eyes will reveal to you how you may proceed in a scene. As Stanislavsky puts it: 'You sit in ambush and follow the smallest movement of your partner. The moment he makes an attempt to go out, stop him, skilfully block his way, interest him in something, surprise him, confuse him' (cited in Toporkov 1998: 86).

• Plant your words in your partner's imagination

As with the Method of Physical Actions, the words used in early improvisations aren't the author's exact text, but the ideas contained within them. The value of the spoken word shouldn't be underestimated in the psycho-physical, improvisational nature of Active Analysis. After all, *verbal action* is just as important as any other. For Stanislavsky, the words mustn't 'lie in the muscles of the tongue', but rather they have to be part of a dynamic process of imparting your own images into the imagination of your partner. Stanislavsky is even quite technical in his notes on verbal actions, stating that, if you want to give the clearest meaning to a line – regardless of the length of a sentence – there should only be one main stress. It's worth paying attention to these notes, as it would be all too easy to consider Active Analysis as something rather hit-and-miss. However, technical precision lies at its very core, in terms of physical, vocal and psychological action. The best touchstone of success with those actions is always your partner and the effect that you have on them: 'just play each action. . . . Check, through your partner's reaction, if you are acting well' (Toporkov 1998: 86). Or not!

THE INSPECTOR GENERAL (1934)

The Inspector General is the third of the productions discussed by Stanislavsky in *Creating a Role*, where yet more of the ideas inherent in Active Analysis are amplified.

* **Never stop training**

Stanislavsky reminds us here that Active Analysis is a rehearsal process, prior to which actors need to have developed their 'inner creative states'. You can't just get up and do it and hope that miraculously your psycho-physical mechanism is fully operational. You need daily, regular actor-training as the ideal accompaniment to rehearsing a play using Active Analysis.

* **Keep it simple**

In your early improvisations, you need very little – you start with your own self and the most basic external facts of the plot. From the 'narrow confines of physical actions', you begin with your own words so that you can 'feel yourself in the part', from where you 'search out their logic and consecutiveness' (Stanislavsky 2000b: 215). As with the Method of Physical Actions, the next step is for the director to prompt you from the sidelines, thereby allowing the author's words to merge gently with your own.

- **Overlay your discoveries with the playwright's text**

The new development of Active Analysis presented with *The Inspector General* is that Stanislavsky suggests compiling *two* lists, one arising intuitively from your improvisations and another list of objectives arising from 'round-the-table analysis' of the play. With the director, you then overlay one list on top of the other, tracing where the two lists coincide and where they diverge. The points at which the two lists are disparate indicate where your own personality is breaking through in a way that is not beneficial to the unfolding of the playwright's text. Therefore, whatever you're doing in these moments needs to be put under the microscope to bring you closer to the line of actions implicit in the original script.

- **Hang on to your objectives**

Keep testing your objectives with the question: 'Why did I do that?' (Stanislavsky 2000b: 226). In this way, the *physical* line of the character will be created in collaboration with its *spiritual* line: in other words, the outer actions ('What am I doing?') and the inner actions ('What do I want?') will totally correspond. (There's a very useful twenty-five point plan of work included as an Appendix to *Creating a Role* (pp. 253–5). Although not all of the points are entirely lucid, it does reveal just how eager Stanislavsky was to try and rationalise the rehearsal process of Active Analysis.)

TARTUFFE (1937)

This is the final production to be looked at briefly in this section, and it is noteworthy because it was the very last experiment that Stanislavsky explored before he died. So, it is the closest indication of where Active Analysis might have been heading. As Stanislavsky continued struggling to articulate a formula for rehearsal, the new idea to be introduced here is a three-step strategy.

Step 1: Reconnaissance

'Reconnaissance' consists (as usual) of analysing separate scenes from the very simple perspective of 'What happened? What took place?'

Underpinning this analysis is a consideration of the through line of action and counteraction of the play as a whole, so that, on behalf of your character, you can ask the questions: 'Where do I stand in relation to this struggle? What is my strategy, my logic of behaviour, my position?' (Toporkov 1998: 164).

Step 2: 'Living through' the events

Step 2 includes making both oral and written accounts of the play and its contents. Although these accounts allow you to analyse the events more deeply, it's important that your descriptions come from the perspective of 'living through' the events. In other words, don't be too objective: keep your descriptions personalised and humanised. As ever, the onus is on the director to ask the right questions, provoking your interest and awakening your imagination.

Step 3: Restraint

Throughout his books, Stanislavsky constantly calls upon actors to 'Cut ninety per cent!' He felt that actors did too much and tried to be too interesting on stage, with the result that very quickly their performances became artificial and insincere. Thus, Step 3 is called 'Restraint'. 'Restraint' in this instance relates to restraining emotions and personal temperament, but more importantly it's about restraining from striving for quick results. Active Analysis is slow and delicate, yet worth pursuing as the results are unexpected, vibrant and genuinely psychophysical.

The stages of improvisations

- **Playing like children**

Toporkov's account of *Tartuffe* provides one of the clearest presentations of how Stanislavsky put the early stages of Active Analysis into practice. At first, the rehearsal space is set out as if it is the house of Orgon, Tartuffe's host. The actors spend time marking out where particular rooms are, and understanding how members of the household function in that space. Improvisations are established of events that aren't in the script, so that the actors are free to play, like children, and stimulate their creative imaginations. These improvisations have titles such as 'Tartuffe Loses His Self-control' and 'The Master of the House goes Mad'. (Toporkov admits that, as they were doing them, the actors thought many of these improvisations were a waste of time. It was only in retrospect, as the elements of the production fell into place, that their value became unquestionable.) Gradually the games suggested by Stanislavsky come closer and closer to the events in the play, though all the time the actors' physical behaviour is more important than their memory of Molière's text.

•   'Communion' between the actors

Even when text is added, a quality of inner improvisation must continue to exist. Stanislavsky reminds the actors that, in life, we usually speak no more than ten per cent of what we're actually feeling or thinking; far more important are our inner actions and ongoing sense of 'communion'. The necessity of communion is made absolutely clear in this section, with Stanislavsky even providing a seven-stage plan of its value:

1   *Orientation*: Your very first step on to the stage needs a moment for you to orientate your character to the given circumstances of the scene.

2   *Searching for the object*: Following this initial moment of orientation, your character then seeks out the object of his or her attention (the 'object' being the reason for which they came into the scene in the first place).

3   *Getting the attention of your partner*: Often the object of attention is another character, whom you need to get in your 'grasp' before the scene can unfold convincingly.

4   *Making contact with your partner*: This involves the interlocking of energies between two actors, which lies at the heart of genuine on-stage communion.

5   *Creating images and making your partner see them as if with your eyes*: This is a matter of playing your objective so potently (without words) that the exchanged energy in itself works upon the other actor. (See exercises below on 'Communion'.)

6   *Thinking only of the images, never of the intonation of the words*: Once words are introduced, you needn't worry about the technical delivery, but simply convey what you want through the playing of actions. If your objective interests you enough, you'll soon find that any strange emphases are eradicated in delivering your text.

7   *Considering how best to transfer those images and events to your partner*: This is a matter of sharpening your inner actions. If you can see that you're not having the desired effect on your partner, you need to invest your objective with even more belief. If you're truly inspired by your objective, you'll soon find that the actions you play on your partner will be difficult for them to ignore.

(adapted from Toporkov 1998: 195)

- **'Communion' with an audience**

A feeling of improvisation doesn't stop at the dress rehearsal. The final element worth noting with *Tartuffe* is the significance that Stanislavsky gives to the live performance. He is still concerned with creating a score of actions, yet 'how I carry out the action according to the score here, before *this* audience – that is creativity' (Stanislavsky cited in Toporkov 1998: 211). In other words, this score isn't fixed. You should be so psycho-physically aware by now that you can adjust your score of actions infinitesimally each night to accommodate the changing nuances of your fellow actors and your unsuspecting audience.

Stanislavsky was undoubtedly a 'master': but there are some very simple ways that we can begin to explore the various components of Active Analysis.

EXERCISES INVOLVING ACTIVE ANALYSIS

Communion or 'irradiation': the Empty Space exercise

Exercise 4.14

Stand opposite your partner at some distance apart. For the duration of the exercise, you must maintain eye contact.

Imagine a coiled spring wound between you both from solar plexus to solar plexus.

Without any overt signals or gestures, and paying limitless attention to every changing nuance in each other's bodies and faces, see if you can find a point of contact. This may be a hug, a slap, a handshake, an embrace, etc.

You may find that one of you moves a great deal, while the other remains almost stationary. You may even find that you never come close enough to establish contact: there is no fixed outcome.

The only consideration is that you sense the changing atmosphere of the space between you as the invisible spring contracts and expands.

In other words, listen to the psycho-physical information that the space itself gives you, as well as that which comes from your partner.

Invariably when this exercise is explained to participants, they can't quite grasp what it's all about. And yet the minute they commit to it, they experience all sorts of sensations, and a vast array of images comes to them.

Silent études

Exercise 4.15

At first, the Empty Space exercise involves no other information than two people and an empty space. However, you can use it as a silent étude if you're rehearsing a playtext through Active Analysis.

First of all, the actors read the scene and determine the basic dramatic structure: What are the inciting and resisting actions? What is the main event without which there would be no encounter?

Then they stand some distance apart (as above), and see if they can find a point of contact, but this time the expansion and contraction of the space between them is informed by the given circumstances that exist between the characters in the play.

Through this simple – silent – encounter, the actors can begin to explore and uncover a mass of psycho-physical information about their characters and about their relationship with the other character.

Of course, further reading and improvisations will uncover all sorts of other details. Nonetheless, the simplicity of this exercise seems to go right to the heart of imaginative freedom, as well as allowing actors to assimilate a mass of information both consciously and unconsciously.

Working with tempo-rhythm

Exercise 4.16

There are all sorts of ways of alerting actors to the power of tempo-rhythm, from playing different pieces of music, to clapping rhythms, to walking in particular tempi. One of the exercises suggested by Stanislavsky in *Building a Character* is good fun!

> A metronome is set and a number of objects are placed on a tray: 'To the deliberate beat of the metronome [Tortsov] had Leo carry the objects away . . . take them from the tray and distribute them to those present' (Stanislavsky 2000a: 200).
>
> Of course, Leo has to justify to himself why he's executing the action at that particular speed.
>
> When Kostya has a go, he imagines that he's the president of some sort of sporting club, distributing ribbons and prizes.
>
> When the tempo-rhythm is increased, Kostya then feels as if he were a butler handing round glasses of champagne at a formal do.
>
> When the tempo-rhythm is again sped up, the image that appears to Kostya is that of a waiter on a train trying to serve everyone before the next stop.
>
> It's then increased a final time, with the result that Kostya feels like the clumsy, clownish Epikhodov in *The Cherry Orchard*.

This is a terrific exercise as, once again, its simplicity allows for a wide range of imaginative suggestions while keeping the basic action the same.

Inner motive forces

Active Analysis is dependent on each actor's inner life (thought, feeling and action) being alert and responsive. In many ways, the broader the individual's life experience, the more material her 'inner motive forces' have at their disposal. But that's not very helpful for the young acting student. Here are some extremely simple exercises to alert the acolyte actor to the potential of the inner motive forces. They also serve as a useful reminder that, within every physical and technical action, there are psychological reverberations. Once again, these exercises stem from the work of Vladimir Ananyev.

Exercise 4.17

In general terms, the thought-centre resides in the head, the emotion-
centre in the chest and the action-centre in the groin.

Explore the room, first of all with the head leading the movement,
then the chest, then the groin.

Instantly, you can feel the different sensations: for example, curiosity
might dominate the first movement, excitement the second and purpose-
fulness the third.

Exercise 4.18

In his book *The Games People Play*, psychologist, Eric Berne, divides
human beings into three different ego states: Adult, Parent and Child.
All of these states exist within each of us, though one state is usually
dominant. These psychological states can be correlated to the 'inner
motive forces', and explored practically through an image and a
movement (see Merlin 2001: 76–80).

The Adult (see Figure 4.3) (associated with the thought-
centre) is holistic, serene and forward-thinking. Picture
yourself standing on a high mountain, seeing over the
landscape as if rays of light are streaming from your
fingertips and all the extremities of your body. When
the image is vivid, start to walk around the room,
noting the sensations caused by the mental
picture.

Figure 4.3
From Point to Space:
the (Holistic) Adult

Figure 4.4 From Point to Point: the (Manipulative) Parent

The Parent (see Figure 4.4) (associated with the emotion-centre) is manipulative. It knows what it wants and how it's going to get there, striving from one place to another like a piece of chalk on a black board. Move around the room, from one point to another, as if this piece of chalk is in your solar plexus. Note what experience that quality of directness conjures up for you.

The Child (see Figure 4.5) (associated with the action-centre) is anarchic. It's like the train of a dress, always following behind the conscious mind. It does something without knowing the consequence. Move around the room with a quality of the train of a dress, exploring the inner sensations inspired by the image and the movement.

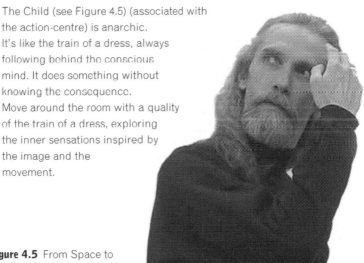

Figure 4.5 From Space to Point: the (Anarchic) Child

After the exercise, the group shares their experiences: usually they find that the tempo-rhythm of the Adult was quite slow and measured, that of the Parent was faster and possibly more staccato, and that of the Child was faster still, constantly changing direction and inner rhythm. It's a useful exercise, as it also catapults the participants' own inner motive forces into action. They experience 'thought' (as the image of each ego-state is given to them), then 'action' (as they put that image into physical vocabulary), and then 'emotion' (as physically exploring each ego-state creates differing emotional responses).

Active Analysis is concerned with psycho-physical processes. This means that, although the exercises listed above can illuminate various aspects of the work, the openness of the approach leaves every teacher and director free to think up their own exercises for unlocking any given scene or emotion. The final note, therefore, is 'Be brave'. Pay absolute attention to the actors' needs within the given circumstances of the play, then let your imagination go!

CONCLUSION

The compactness of this book can't accommodate all the events and roles which preoccupied Stanislavsky and unquestionably affected his developing 'system'. So readers are strongly advised to turn to some of the wonderful books and biographies that are available, not least of which are Jean Benedetti's *Stanislavski: His Life and Art* (1999) and Sharon M. Carnicke's *Stanislavsky in Focus* (1998). These elaborate on various theories and ideas touched upon here. However, the aim here has been to trace the main strands of Stanislavsky's 'system' and production practice, from his early amateur cavortings to his deathbed, dispelling a few myths along the way. In seeing how his ideas form a mesh, toing and froing across the chronology of his life, we quickly realise that his final legacies – the Method of Physical Actions and Active Analysis – were inevitable. And they're still highly provocative and liberating approaches to stage production.

While Stanislavsky and his 'system' are certainly not the be-all and end-all of modern acting practice, many theatre pioneers – from Grotowski to Brook to Barba and beyond – have drawn upon his ideas. By using his writings as a springboard into our own experiments, we can prevent them from stagnating into history books. Whether our preferences lie in physical theatre, postmodern dance or the realism of film and television, we'll never escape the fact that we are nothing but body, imagination, emotions and spirit: acting will always be psycho-physical to a greater or lesser extent. There can be no question that Stanislavsky was the first twentieth-century practitioner to investigate it seriously.

A BRIEF GLOSSARY
OF TERMS

action 7

Every moment that the actor is on stage and every line of text spoken consists of an action. It is directed towards the other characters in the scene, and is usually expressed as a transitive verb ('I persuade you', 'I threaten you', 'I enchant you', etc.). Each action is like a bead: if you string the beads together, you have your character's through line of action, which then propels and guides you through the entire play.

Active Analysis 25

This was the rehearsal process that Stanislavsky was exploring at the time of his death and that was subsequently developed by his students and assistants. At its heart lies improvisation, with the actors taking whatever information they have 'Here, Today, Now' as the starting point for creative work. Through the simple sequence of reading the text, discussing and improvising, they find that their words and **actions** move closer and closer to the playwright's script, with the formal learning of text reduced to a minimum.

activity 10

This is a piece of stage 'business' of a relatively simple nature which can underscore the dialogue of a play, such as the lotto game in

Act 4 of *The Seagull*. It's not dissimilar to a **physical action**, though Grotowski illustrates how an activity can easily become a physical action with the correct psychological justification. Thus, 'you can ask me a very embarrassing question, so . . . I stall for a time, I begin then to solidly prepare my pipe. Now my activity becomes a physical action, because it becomes my weapon' (Grotowski cited in Richards 1995: 74).

affective memory 4

(Also known as 'emotion memory' or 'sense memory'.) This term describes the process of recalling situations from your own experience (including events that you've read about, heard about, or seen, as well as directly experienced) that are analogous to the character's situation. It involves the collaborative work of the imagination and all your senses (taste, touch, sight, smell and hearing) in the recalling of incidents. Finding an appropriate affective memory is a means of empathising with the contents of a play so that you can invest them with something from your personal landscape. This process of empathy should prevent your characterisations becoming clichéd and formal.

bit 16

This term is frequently translated as 'unit'. A bit or 'unit' is a section of text in which the characters are clearly pursuing a particular **objective**. At the point at which one character's objective is thwarted or achieved, a new dynamic usually begins and so a new bit starts. A bit of text may be as short as two lines of dialogue or as long as two pages. A character's exit from or entrance into a scene tends to delineate the end of one bit and the start of the next. The label for a bit needn't be an active verb in the way that both **actions** and objectives demand. So the heading for a bit of text might be, for example: 'The Seduction', 'Casing the Joint', or 'Follow my Leader'.

communion 21

Despite sounding somewhat esoteric, communion is in fact incredibly simple. It is the absolute attention of one actor to another, primarily through eye contact, though also through the exchange of energy which inevitably takes place between two or more human beings. It involves each actor getting the other actor in his or her

grasp. Every facial gesture, every physical movement, every sound, is instantaneously noted and responded to by each actor leading to a constant state of inner (and outer) improvisation. If the actors are 'in each other's grasp', the audience will be drawn – like magnets – towards the on-stage action. In this way, they also became part of the communion or grasp of the live performance.

emotion memory *see* **affective memory**

given circumstances 16   These are all the pieces of information needed by actors to make the appropriate decisions when interpreting their characters. They include 'the story of the play, its facts, events, epoch, time and place of action, conditions of life, the actors' and *regisseurs*' interpretation, the *mise-en-scène*, the production, the sets, the costumes, properties, lighting and sound effects' (Stanislavsky 1980: 51).

grasp 65   When two or more actors are fully engaged with each other – through eye contact or aural listening or through acute attention to the nuances and changes in each other's performances – then they are in each other's grasp. It is a vital and exciting state of connection and **communion**, which allows for constant inner improvisation in each actor. Such playful performances, steeped in the **given circumstances** of the playtext and the director's *mise-en-scène*, can draw the audience dynamically towards the live action on stage.

inner motive forces 24   These are the three main components of the actor's psycho-physical instrument: intellect (thought-centre), feelings (emotion centre) and the physical manifestation of those thoughts and feelings through the body (will- or action-centre). The spontaneous dialogues that exist between these three centres lie at the heart of psycho-physical acting processes.

life of the human spirit 11   Stanislavsky believed that actors could go beyond the limits of their own personalities into a highly textured and powerful manifestation of a character. To do this, they placed themselves 'in the very thick of [their character's] imagined life' (Stanislavsky 1984: 171), by analysing the text, by fully imagining the **given circumstances** of the play and by having 'a good command of emotional and physical techniques' (ibid.). In other words, the actors drew upon their emotional, physical, technical and spiritual resources to create the life of the human spirit for their role. This would give their characterisation 'the highest power of impact' and 'the highest degree of receptivity from the audience' (ibid.: 171–2).

Method of Physical Actions 18   Following on from his round-the-table detective work, Stanislavsky found that the actual living bodies and imaginations of his actors themselves could unlock the intricacies of a text quickly and inventively. The rehearsal process underlying the Method of Physical Actions is concerned with finding a logical and coherent 'score of physical actions' that takes the actors from simple external **activities** into complex psychological experiences.

moment of orientation 142   It's very easy when you're familiar with a play to find yourself taking moments for granted on stage. For example, when you enter an on-stage room, you know exactly where the other characters are going to be and unconsciously you begin to iron out all the unexpected components that happen in real life. The moment of orientation, then, is that first moment when you enter the stage: it is a moment in which you take stock of where you are, to whom you're speaking, what your **objective** for coming into the room was, and what actions you are going to execute on the other characters in order to achieve your objective. Although it is literally only a moment, the moment of orientation can be the deciding factor in what constitutes a credible and spontaneous performance, rather than one which betrays the fact that the actors have pre-arranged everything.

objective 16   The actual translation of this word is 'task'. An objective is the main desire motivating a character's behaviour in a scene or within a particular **bit**, and it is directed towards the on-stage partner. Like **actions**, the objective is expressed through an active verb, with a phrase beginning 'I wish to . . .' or 'I want to . . .'. Labelling an objective needs attention as, according to Stanislavsky, it 'must call up not just simple interest but passionate excitement, desires, aspirations and actions' (Stanislavsky 2000b: 63).

pause 16   Far from being a moment of inactivity, a pause is full of inner **action** and emotional intensity. It is the silent, inner continuation of one action and the preparation for a new action. Stanislavsky divides the use of pauses into two categories. The 'logical pause' comes at the end of a line and a stanza, giving literary sense and intelligibility to a text. The 'psychological pause' can appear anywhere, as long as it is necessary and breathes life into the text, as we can see in the production plan of *The Seagull*. Pauses serve actors in two ways: (1) during actor-training, they provide the chance to monitor what is going on inside the actors in terms of their inner processes; in this way, actors can begin to develop a creative consciousness; and (2) in performance, as the infant Moscow Art Theatre discovered with *The Seagull*, pauses encourage the actors to connect with the rest of the ensemble in terms of silent **communion**.

physical action 19   A physical action is basically an inner or outer action which carries with it a psychological motivation. It is a blend of **action**, **objective** and **activity**. In other words, it's a small achievable **task** full of psychological reverberations designed to affect the on-stage partner and the dramatic situation. Grotowski sums up the distinction between a simple movement and a physical action: 'If I am walking towards the door, it is not an action but a movement. But if I am walking towards the door to "contest your stupid questions", to threaten you that I will break up the conference, there will be a cycle of little actions and not just a movement' (cited in Richards 1995: 76).

sense memory *see* **affective memory**

subtext 97
This term refers to the motivations which underlie the surface of the spoken text and external **action**. A character's subtext can be expressed through specific intonation, looks, gestures, **pauses**, or stillness. As Stanislavsky puts it: 'Keep in mind that a person says only ten per cent of what lies in his head, ninety per cent remains unspoken. On the stage [we] forget this, [we] are concerned only with what is said aloud, and thereby destroy the living truth. Playing any scene, you should first create all the thoughts which precede this or that cue. You don't have to express them but you have to live with them' (cited in Toporkov 1998: 181).

super-objective 42

This is the goal towards which each character journeys throughout the play. The playwright has a super-objective, as does the play itself, as well as each of the characters in the play. A play's super-objective will unite the playwright, the director, the actors and all the characters within the play. It works together with the through line of action. Thus:

> the super-objective and the through action represent creative goal and creative action, which contain in themselves all the thousands of separate, fragmentary objectives, units, action in a role. The super-objective is the quintessence of the play. The through line of action is the *leitmotif* which runs through the entire work. Together they guide the creativeness and strivings of the actor.
>
> (Stanislavsky 2000b: 79).

task *see* objective

tempo-rhythm 91

'Tempo' is the speed at which an **action** is performed and 'rhythm' is the intensity with which the action is performed. A character's *inner* tempo-rhythm may contrast with the speed and intensity with which the *outer* **activities** are performed. As Stanislavsky pin-points, Chekhov's characters 'are almost always outwardly calm while inwardly throbbing with emotional turmoil' (Stanislavsky 2000a: 212). Tempo-rhythm has the power to stir the actors' emotions and arouse striking visual images and memories. So it's worth spending time locating a character's tempo-rhythm, as it can often provide the actor with a fantastic trigger into the character's psychology. Again, Stanislavsky's advice is:

> Listen to how your emotions tremble, throb, race, are stirred inside you. In these invisible movements lie hidden all manner of rapid and slow beats, hence tempi and rhythms. Every human passion, every state of being, every experience has its tempo-rhythm. Every characteristic inner or external image has its own tempo-rhythm.
>
> (2000a: 198)

unit *see* bit

SELECTED BIBLIOGRAPHY

Allen, D. (1999) *Stanislavski For Beginners*, London: Writers & Readers.

Balukhaty, S. D. (ed.) (1952) The Seagull *Produced by Stanislavsky*, trans. David Magarshack, London: Dobson.

Benedetti, J. (1990) *Stanislavski: A Biography*, London: Methuen.

Benedetti, J. (1991) *The Moscow Art Theatre Letters*, London: Methuen.

Benedetti, J. (1994) *Stanislavski: An Introduction*, London: Methuen.

Benedetti, J. (1999) *Stanislavski: His Life and Art*, London: Methuen.

Berne, E. (1964) *Games People Play: The Psychology of Human Relationships*, London: Penguin

Boleslavsky, R. (1933) *Acting: The First Six Lessons*, New York: Theater Arts Books.

Carnicke, S. M. (1998) *Stanislavsky in Focus*, Amsterdam: Harwood Academic Publishers.

Chekhov, A. (1990) *The Seagull*, trans. Michael Frayn, London: Methuen.

Cole, T. (ed.) (1983) *Acting: A Handbook of the Stanislavski Method*, New York: Crown.

Cousin, G. (1982) 'Stanislavsky and Brecht: The Relationship between the Actor and Stage Objects', unpublished thesis, Exeter: University of Exeter.

Edwards, C. (1966) *The Stanislavski Heritage: Its Contribution to the Russian and American Theatre*, London: Peter Owen.

Gauss, R. B. (1999) *Lear's Daughters: The Studios of the Moscow Art Theatre 1905–1927*, New York: Peter Lang.

Gorchakov, N. M. (1994) *Stanislavski Directs*, trans. Miriam Goldina, New York: Limelights.

Gordon, M. (1987) *The Stanislavski Technique: Russia: A Workbook for Actors*, New York: Applause.

Hodge, A. (ed.) (2000) *Twentieth Century Actor Training*, London: Routledge.

Knebel, M. (1981) 'On Analysis through Action of a Play and a Role', trans. Alma Law, unpublished paper.

Leach, R. (2003) *Stanislavsky and Meyerhold*, Bern: Peter Lang AG.

Leach, R. and Borovsky, V. (eds) (1999) *A History of Russian Theatre*, Cambridge: Cambridge University Press.

Leiter, S. (1991) *From Stanislavsky to Barrault: Representative Directors of the European Stage*, New York: Greenwood Press.

Lewis, Robert (1986) *Method – or Madness?*, London: Methuen.

Magarshack, D. (1950) *Stanislavsky: A Life*, London: Faber & Faber.

Melchinger, S. (1972) *Anton Chekhov*, New York: Ungar.

Merlin, B. (2001) *Beyond Stanislavsky: The Psycho-physical Approach to Actor Training*, London: Nick Hern Books.

Mitter, S. (1993) *Systems of Rehearsal: Stanislavsky, Brecht, Grotowski and Brook*, London: Routledge.

Moore, S. (ed.) (1973) *Stanislavski Today: Commentaries on K. S. Stanislavski*, New York: American Center for Stanislavski Theater Art.

Moore, S. (1979) *Stanislavski Revealed: The Actor's Guide to Spontaneity on Stage*, New York: Applause.

Moore, S. (1984) *The Stanislavski System: The Professional Training of an Actor*, New York: Penguin.

Nemirovich-Danchenko, V. (1937) *My Life in the Russian Theatre*, trans. John Cournos, Boston: Little, Brown & Co.

Richards, T. (1995) *At Work with Grotowski on Physical Actions*, London: Routledge.

Schuler, C. (1996) *Women in the Russian Theatre*, London: Routledge.

Stafford-Clark, M. (1990) *Letters to George*, London: Nick Hern Books.

Stanislavsky, K. (1938) *Chayka: V Postanovke, Regissers Kaya Partitura Stanislavskovo*, Leningrad: Isskustvo.

Stanislavsky, K. (1948) *Stanislavsky Produces* Othello, trans. Dr Helen Nowak, London: Geoffrey Bles.

Stanislavsky, K. (1958) *Stanislavsky's Legacy: Comments on Some Aspects of an Actor's Art and Life*, trans. Elizabeth Reynolds Hapgood, London: Max Reinhardt.

Stanislavsky, K. (1973) *On the Art of the Stage*, trans. David Magarshack, London: Faber & Faber.

Stanislavsky, K. (1980) *An Actor Prepares*, trans. Elizabeth Reynolds Hapgood, London: Methuen (first published in Britain 1937).

Stanislavsky, K. (1982) *My Life in Art*, trans. J. J. Robbins, London: Methuen (first published 1924).

Stanislavsky, K. (1984) *Selected Works*, trans. Vladimir Yankilevsky, Moscow: Raduga.

Stanislavsky, K. (1990) *An Actor's Handbook*, trans. Elizabeth Reynolds Hapgood, London: Methuen.

Stanislavsky, K. (2000a) *Building a Character*, trans. Elizabeth Reynolds Hapgood, London: Methuen.

Stanislavsky, K. (2000b) *Creating a Role*, trans. Elizabeth Reynolds Hapgood, London: Methuen.

Stanislavsky, K. and Rumyantsev, P. (1998) *Stanislavski on Opera*, trans. Elizabeth Reynolds Hapgood, New York: Routledge.

Styan, J. L. (1984) *Realism and Naturalism: Modern Drama in Theory and Practice Volume 1*, Cambridge: Cambridge University Press.

Toporkov, V. O. (1998) *Stanislavski in Rehearsal: The Final Years*, London: Routledge.

Worrall, N. (1996) *The Moscow Art Theatre*, London: Routledge.

INDEX

Numbers in bold type indicate pages containing illustrations.